295
Michaels
$950
AF576403
Gran's Garden
By Ros Stallcup
Susan Scheewe Publications Inc.

FERN BASKET
Pages 47, 48, 49

THROUGH THE ARBOR
Pages 36, 37, 38, 47

GERANIUM GARDEN SET
Pages 50, 51

SUNFLOWER GARDEN SET
Pages 17, 18, 19

ANGEL BABY OUTFIT
Pages 58, 59, 60, 61

BABY SHIRT
Pages 62, 63

13435 N.E. Whitaker Way, Portland, Oregon 97230
Phone (503) 254-9100

About the Author

I have been a member of Susan Scheewe National Teaching Staff since 1982, traveling and teaching painting seminars in the Mid Atlantic states at a hectic pace all these years. My husband tells everyone that I am "leaving tomorrow and will be home in November." It has been a wonderful experience. I have met so many people, shop owners and students alike, and I feel I have made friends for life.
I have watched their children grow up and some have made me member of their family. Painting and teaching has brought many special things into my life and I am glad to have an opportunity to share some of these things with you.

I would like to dedicate this book to Sue Scheewe and all my team sisters who have put up with me and encouraged me all these years. With Sue's help and support this book will be a reality. Thank you all.

Writing this book has been a challenge for me. I have become on speaking terms with our computer and have learned about a *Passive Sentence.* Thank goodness for a spell checker. The painted pieces have been fun as I have had little time to paint things just for me in years. One project led to another. I keep waking up at 4 am hatching up new projects. I will never finish.

Ros Stallcup
1436 Lakeview Dr.
Virginia Beach, Va. 23455

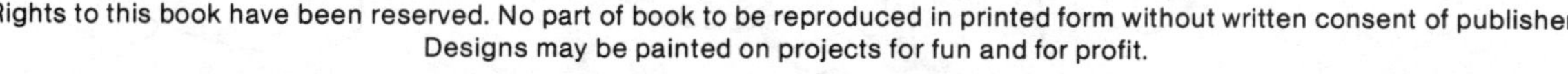

Supplies

Paints - Listed in each project

I have used Deco Americana acrylic paints and Grumbacher fabric dyes. Conversion charts used in this book are only guides to colors. Always refer to the color pictures. There are many variations of colors. For red , as an example, anything close to the color red will work. It doesn't have to be exactly the same shade of red.

Brushes - Synthetic

Flats - # 4, 12 and 20
Round - # 2 and 6
Liner - # 1
Angular Shader 1/4", 3/8' and 1/2"
Filbert (Cat's Tongue) - # 4 and 8
Susie's Foliage Brush - 3/4" or angular bristle brush.

I used Grumbacher Control Plus,Grumbacher Golden Edge and Stan Brown's Brushes.

General Supplies

- Water container
- Masking tape 1/4" and wider (3 M recommended.)
- Tack rag
- Wood filler
- Acrylic palette paper
- Pigma Pens (extra fine point permanent marker). Recommended.
- Or Rapidograph Technical Pens with Rapidograph #3080 Universal Ink
- Paper Towels
- Stylus or a red ink ball-point pen
- Tracing paper
- Graphite Paper - White and Gray
- #400 Sandpaper
- White Lightening or other wood sealer
- J.W. Right Step waterbased varnish
- Misket

SMALL BIRDHOUSES
Scheewe Publications Inc.
13435 N.E. Whitaker Way
Portland, Or. 97230
503-254-9100 PH
503-252-9508 FAX

Wood Sources

Stan Brown's Arts and Crafts
13435 E. Whitaker Way
Portland, Or. 97230

Walnut Hollow Farms
Rt. 2
Dodgeville, Wi. 53533

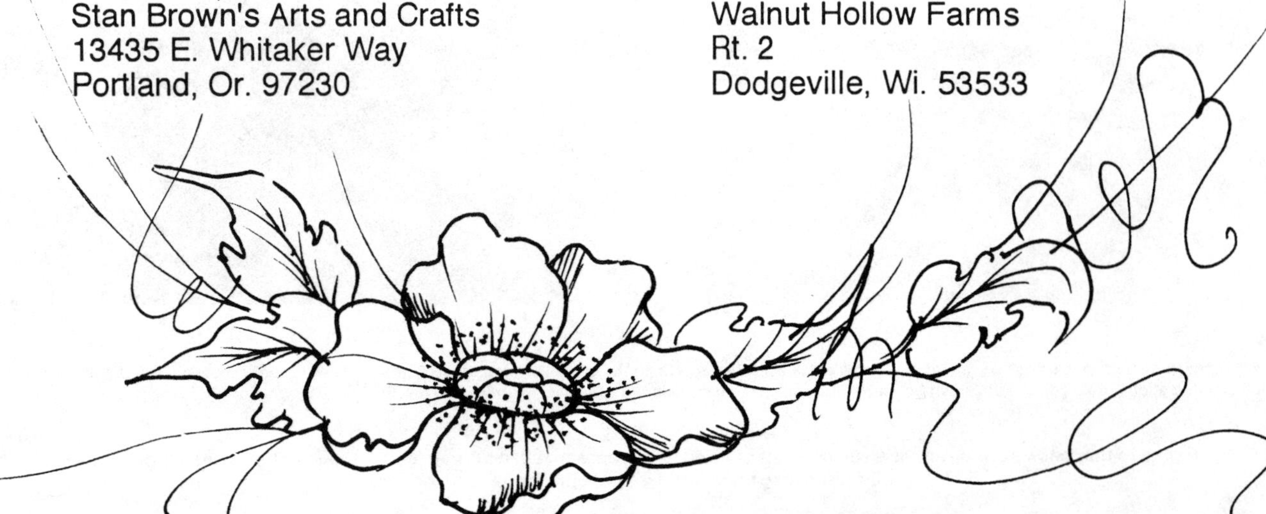

Painting with Acrylic

I Have used Deco Americana paint on these projects. If you prefer another brand of paints refer to the interchange chart.

Some definitions may help.

Basecoat - To apply the first layer of color.

Shading and Highlighting - To apply color on top of the base coat, both dark and light to give dimension to your painting.

Detailing - To add fine lines, flower centers, stems, and other touches to give a finished look to your painting.

Tapping - To tap very lightly using the tip of the brush, bouncing around rather than moving in straight rows. Use this technique to create foliage or flowers.

Painting Flowers

Brushes must be in good shape to paint flower petals. The brush is doing most of the work so take really good care of them. If you are consistantly unhappy with your results consider a new brush. Practice Practice Practice

Misket

A blocking agent used in watercolor. Protect your paint brush when using Misket by brushing the wet hairs back and forth across the surface of a bar of soap. Keep the soap up in the metal ferrule of the brush and dip into the Misket. Wash your brush out with soap and water as soon as you finish.

Helpful Hints

Painting is something you do alone, for yourself, so remember to have fun. Follow your own instincts about color and form. Don't be afraid to experiment with other colors as there are many colors found in our gardens. This book is only a guide to some techniques that may help you to accomplish these and other projects.

Many of the flowers in this book are the ones that grow in my garden. Try to paint the flowers that grow in your garden.

Be patient with yourself. Practice will make a big difference. If you are not happy with what you have painted then just re-paint it! Rubbing alcohol removes areas of dry acrylic from sealed wood. Now do it again, and again, until your results satisfy you.

Paint small fine lines using a liner brush and a little water to extend your paint. Put the least amount of pressure you can on the tip of your brush. If painted small fine lines are not your thing then try inking them on top of your dry paint.

Keep your brushes clean! Acrylic will dry quickly up in the ferrule of your brushes. While you are painting keep your brushes in water and clean them out thoroughly before you lay them down.

Basic Wood Preparation

Fill any holes with wood filler and let them dry completely. Sand level. I have used White Lightning as a base coat on all my pieces as it is also a great sealer. Leave the white-washed effect of White Lightning or add another coat with acrylic color. Let the base coat dry completely and then sand lightly with 400 or *fine* sand paper. The final finish should feel smooth but not slick to the touch.

Basic Preparation Clay Flower Pots

Use only new clay pots. Spray with a coat of clear Krylon Matte inside and out, to seal surface. Allow to dry.
Paint two coats of acrylic, inside and out, using a large flat brush or sponge brush. Pattern and paint. When complete varnish with two coat of Right Step water based varnish.

Use an watertight inner liner as clay pots are porous. Moisture seeping through the pot may damage the painted surface.

Tin or Galvanized Preparation

Surface must be clean and free of rust. Sand lightly to rough surface and spray with metal primer. Allow to dry and paint with two coats of acrylic.

Transferring Patterns on Wood or Other Firm Surface

Trace pattern on to tracing paper. Position tracing paper pattern on surface and anchor in place using masking tape. Place graphite paper underneath the tracing paper pattern with dark side down. Transfer basic lines by retracing the pattern using a stylist or ball point pen. I like to use a red ball point pen so I can see which lines I have traced. Always check as you get started to see that the lines are transferring properly. Take your time; a clear, crisp pattern is worth the extra few minutes.

Transferring Patterns to Soft Fabric or Sweatshirt

Trace pattern onto tulle (a fine nylon netting) using a permanent marking pen. Position tulle tracing on the fabric or sweat shirt and again hold in place with masking tape. In the case of wearable art it is always wise to check placement of design by trying it on or looking in a mirror. Retrace the design through the tulle using a charcoal pencil, white or black, depending on the color of your fabric.

Patterning Straw Hats

Use the tulle method. Transfer with a soft pencil graphite pencil

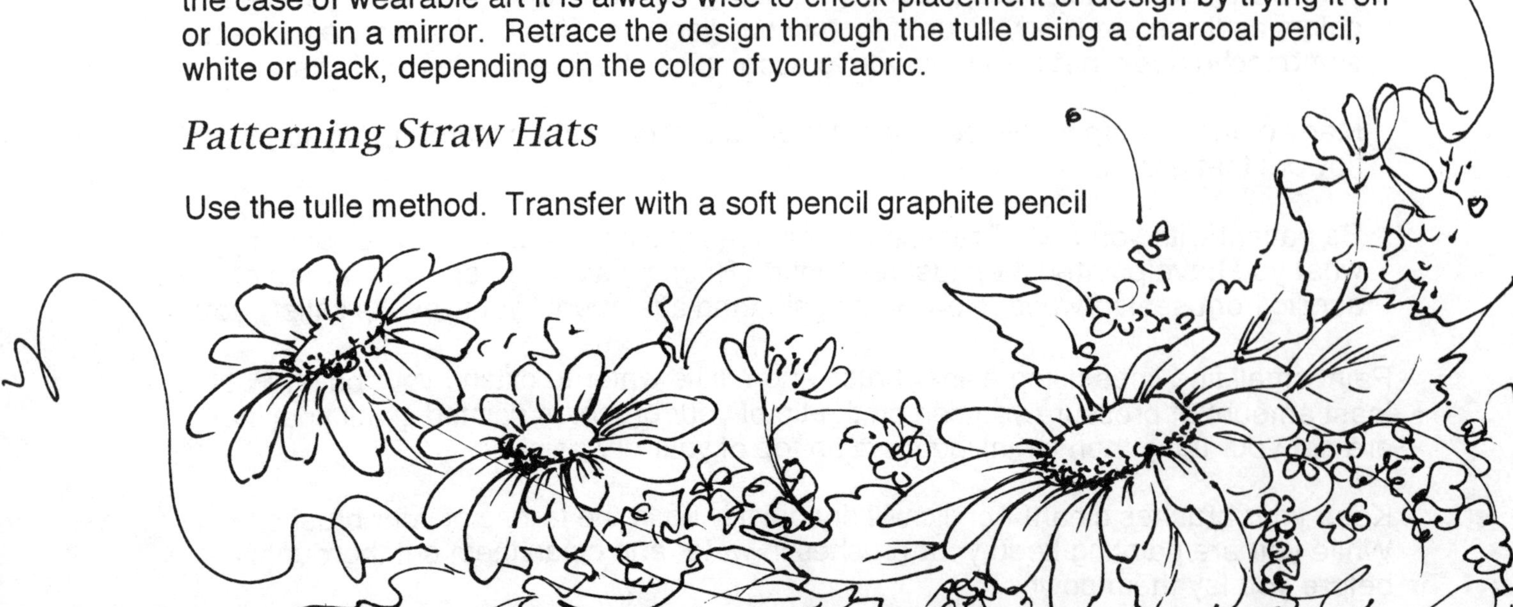

Inking on Fabric or Wood

Use either a Rapidograph Technical Pen (size 0) and Universal Ink (No. 3080) or a Pigma pen (size .05).

Transfer pattern to fabric or wood tracing only basic lines. Ink the design adding as many extra lines as desired.

One method is to paint your object first then, when it is dry, ink little stems, squiggles and detail lines on top of the paint. The ink is permanent on top of acrylic and fabric dye.

Painting on Fabric

Fabric Dyes:

I use the Grumbacher Fabric Dyes. Fabric dyes penetrate the fabric and the colors are clear and crisp. Use these dyes like watercolors by adding water or textile medium. Each fabric will take water and paint differently so experiment to find what works best for your project. The Grumbacher Fabric Dyes come in Galaxy colors which are iridescence and Designer colors which are flat. I have used both.

Textile Medium:

Use textile medium to extend your paint and to help the paint penetrate the fabric. I use it when I want a watercolor effect and want to prevent the colors from running together. For example, when painting a large flower, first base the edges of a petal with textile medium then wet the rest of the petal with a small amount of water. Apply a small amount of paint to the damp surface. This allows you to shade darker streaks near center of the flower and edges, while leaving some of your background color showing. The textile medium will stops the petal color from running beyond the edges of the flower.

Fabrics:

Fabrics made of cotton and synthetic blends are best for painting as they tend not fade or shrink. Smooth surface fabrics are easiest to pattern and paint. After your painting is dry and has cured for at least two days, heat set your design by putting it in the clothes dryer. Turn your garment inside out and set dryer on high for about 10 minutes.

The garden gloves I have painted on came from the hardware store and have a logo printed across the back of one of them. Paint a coat of white across the logo and let it dry. Paint over it and you do not need to worry about it showing through.

Color Comparison Chart

All symbols key on the DecoArt color:
A (+) by another company's color means that the color family is the same, but the other company's color is darker than DecoArt.
A (-) by another company's color means that the color family is the same, but the other company's color is lighter than DecoArt.
An (*) by the DecoArt color means that no other company has a reasonably comparative color to our knowledge.

These comparisons were compared dry to dry. As some companies vary their colors slightly in different batches, please be aware that the colors will be close but seldom exact. This color comparison chart is as close as representative samples as possible, however, DecoArt does not guarantee the identical color matches of competitive colors. This is only a general guide for comparison.

COLORS	DECOART AMERICANA (DA)	DELTA CERAMCOAT	PLAID FOLKART	ILLINOIS BRONZE ACCENT & COUNTRY COLORS
WHITES	DA1 Snow White		901 Wicker White	2476 Real White
	DA2 White Wash	E White		2454 White Wash
	DA3 Buttermilk	2001 Antique White	903 Tapioca	2428 Off White
	DA4 Sand	2036 Ivory	902 Taffy	2311 Adobe Wash
	DA77 Desert Sand		703 Vanilla Cream	
	DA89 Cool Neutral	2402 Sandstone	857 Porcelain White	
	DA90 Warm Neutral		704 Milkshake	
YELLOWS	(*)DA5 Taffy Cream			
	DA6 Pineapple	2005 Pale Yellow		2306 Cactus Flower
	(*)DA7 Moon Yellow			
	DA8 Yellow Ochre	(-)2092 Old Parchment	737 Butter Crunch	
	DA9 Antique Gold	2003 Oaktone		
	DA10 Cadmium Yellow	D Yellow		736 School Bus Yellow
	DA11 Lemon Yellow	2064 Sunbright Yellow	(+)918 Sunny Yellow	2410 Mellow Yellow
		(+)2027 Bright Yellow	735 Lemon Custard	
		2004 Luscious Lemon		
		(-)2101 Pineapple		
	(*)DA93 Raw Sienna			
ORANGES	DA12 Tangerine	2028 Native Flesh		
		2042 Pumpkin		
	DA13 Pumpkin	(+)2026 Orange		2473 True Orange
		(+)2043 Tangerine		
	DA14 Cadmium Orange		920 Autumn Leaves	2573 Floral Orange
	(*)DA15 Cadmium Red			
	DA16 Burnt Orange	2097 Georgia Clay		
	DA17 Georgia Clay	2030 Burnt Sienna		
		2020 Red Iron Oxide		
	DA102 Medium Flesh	2126 Medium Flesh		2420 Peaches 'n Cream

COLORS	DECOART AMERICANA (DA)	DELTA CERAMCOAT	PLAID FOLKART	ILLINOIS BRONZE ACCENT & COUNTRY COLORS
REDS	DA18 Country Red	2098 Tomato Spice	931 Red Clay	2302 Pueblo Red
	DA19 Berry Red	2107 Tompt Red	932 Calico Red	2470 Pure Red
				2449 Jo Sonja Red
	DA20 Calico Red	C Bright Red		2579 Razzle Red
	DA21 Crimson Tide	2075 Maroon	758 Cherry Royale	2332 Bordeauz
			935 Raspberry Wine	2421 Holiday Red
	DA22 Burgundy Wine	2130 Sweetheart Blush	(-)957 Burgundy	
		2125 Pthalo Crimson		
	DA79 Brandy Wine	2123 Burgundy Rose	847 Apple Spice	
	DA80 Russet	2407 Candy Bar	757 Brownie	
	DA96 Red Iron Oxide	2020 Red Iron Oxide	914 Rusty Nail	2424 Barn Red
	DA97 Rookwood Red	2446 Sonoma	756 Chocolate Cherry	2425 Fingerberry Red
	(*)DA104 Napthol Red	2408 Napthol Crimson		
	DA112 Cranberry Wine		935 Raspberry Wine	
PINKS MAUVES PURPLES	DA23 Peaches & Cream	(-)2433 Island Coral	(+)911 Apricot Cream	2319 L 'Orangerie
	DA24 Flesh	(-)2033 Dresden Flesh		
	DA25 Dusty Rose	(-)2018 Indiana Rose	752 Berries 'N Cream	2452 Victorian Mauve
		2432 Normandy Rose	(-)929 Cotton Candy	
	DA26 Mauve	2132 Bouquet	753 Rose Chiffon	2450 Roseberry
	DA27 Gooseberry	2129 Gypsy Rose	(-)912 Promenade	
	DA28 Raspberry	2405 Dusty Mauve		
	(*)DA29 Boysenberry			
	DA30 Spice Pink		955 Sweetheart Pink	
	(*)DA31 Baby Pink			
	(*)DA32 Lilac			
	DA33 Orchid	(+)2403 Lilac Dust		
		2060 Lilac		
	DA34 Lavender		(-)933 Heather	2475 True Purple
				2304 Purple Canyon
	DA101 Dioxazine Purple	2015 Purple		
	DA103 Coral Rose	2045 Fiesta Pink		
	DA110 Blush			

COLORS	DECOART AMERICANA (DA)	DELTA CERAMCOAT	PLAID FOLKART	ILLINOIS BRONZE ACCENT & COUNTRY COLORS
BLUES	DA35 Navy Blue	2114 Midnight	908 Indigo	2446 Indigo Blue
	DA36 True Blue	(-)2124 Manganese Blue		2472 Pure Blue
		2089 Navy Blue		2412 Ultra Marine Blue
		2051 Copen Blue		
		B Phalo Blue		
	DA37 Blueberry	2131 Nightfall		
	(*)DA38 Wedgewood Blue			
	DA39 Victorian Blue			(-)2563 Larkspur Blue
	DA40 Williamsburg Blue	(-)2069 Wedgewood Blue		2440 Stoneware Blue
		2133 Cape Cod		
	(*)DA41 Country Blue			
	DA42 Baby Blue	2037 Blue Heaven		
	(*)DA43 Salem Blue			
	DA44 Desert Turquoise	2058 Colonial Blue		
	DA81 Colonial Green			2451 Village Green
	DA85 Midnight Blue	2413 Prusian Blue	964 Midnight	2439 Liberty Blue
	DA86 Uniform Blue	2114 Midnight	(+)975 Slate Blue	2441 Soldier Blue
	DA87 Indian Turquoise		722 Baby Blue	(+)2307 Nevada Turquoise
	DA98 French Blue	2133 Cape Cod		2440 Stoneware Blue
	(*)DA99 Sapphire			
	DA100 Ultra Deep Blue	2038 Ultra Marine Blue		
	DA105 Blue Grey Mist		718 Blue Gray Dust	
	DA115 Blue Haze			2310 Prairie Green
GREENS	DA45 Mint Julep		(+)915 Robin's Egg	
	(*)DA46 Sea Aqua			
	DA47 Bluegrass Green	2115 Blue Spruce		
	DA48 Holly Green	2068 Christmas Green		2577 Holiday Green
	DA49 Dark Pine	2100 Woodland Night	725 Tartan Green	2310 Prairie Green
	(*)DA50 Forest Green			
	DA51 Leaf Green	2420 Dark Jungle	927 Old Ivy	2442 Green Olive
			926 Shamrock	
	DA52 Avacado	2420 Dark Jungle	952 Ripe Avocado	2320 Chateau Moss
			(-)928 Patchwork Green	
			(-)923 Clover	
GREENS	DA53 Mistletoe	2011 Chrome Greebn Lt.		
	(*)DA54 Bright Green			
	DA55 Kelly Green	2008 Green Isle		
	DA56 Olive Green	2067 Leaf Green	954 Fresh Foliage	
	DA57 Jade Green	(+)2422 Leprechaun	922 Bayberry	
		2070 Wedgewood Green		
	DA82 Evergreen	2010 Forest Green	924 Thicket	2445 Pine Needle Green
	DA83 Black Forest	2096 Dark Forest	727 Parrot Green	2444 Deep Forest Green
	DA84 Midnight Green	2116 Black Green	925 Wrought Iron	
	DA106 Lt. Avocado		728 Green Olive	2438 Chesapeake Blue
	(*)DA108 Viridian Green	A Pthalo Green		
	DA113 Plantation Pine		730 Southern Pine	
	DA116 Deep Teal			2438 Chesapeake Blue

COLORS	DECOART AMERICANA (DA)	DELTA CERAMCOAT	PLAID FOLKART	ILLINOIS BRONZE ACCENT & COUNTRY COLORS
BROWNS	DA58 Antique White	(-)2402 Sandstone	(+)939 Butter Pecan	2453 Wicker
	DA59 Toffee	2085 AC Flesh		
	DA60 Mocha	(-)2019 Fleshtone		
	DA61 Sable Brown	2425 Territorial Beige		
	DA62 Terra Cotta	(+)2055 Autumn Brown		
		2086 Toffee		
	DA63 Burnt Sienna	2023 Brown Iron Oxide	945 Maple Syrup	2435 Burnt Sienna
			943 Molasses	
	DA64 Burnt Umber	2053 Dark Brown	940 Coffee Bean	2408 Sweet Chocolate
	DA65 Dark Chocolate	2024 Walnut	950 Chocolate Fudge	2437 Burnt Umber
		2025 Burnt Umber		
	DA78 Flesh Tone	2125 Medium Flesh	949 Skintone	
	DA91 Cashmere Beige	2033 Dresden Flesh	705 Almond Parfait	
	DA92 Mink Tan	2424 Bambi	706 Chocolait Parfait	
	DA94 Mississippi Mud	2109 Brown Velvet		2436 Raw Sienna
	DA109 Taupe			
	DA114 Lt. Cinnamon			
BLACKS GREYS	DA67 Ebony Black	F Black	938 Licorice	2477 Real Black
	(*)DA88 Charcoal Grey			
	(*)DA68 Slate Grey			
	DA69 Dove Grey	(+)2425 Cadet Grey		
	(*)DA95 Neutral Grey	2090 Hippo Grey		
	DA111 Grey Sky			
METALLICS	DA70 Shimmering Silver		No Comparable Product	
	DA71 Glorious Gold		No Comparable Product	
	DA72 Venetian Gold		No Comparable Product	
	DA73 Bronze		No Comparable Product	
	DA74 Royal Ruby		No Comparable Product	
	DA75 Ice Blue		No Comparable Product	
	DA76 Crystal Green		No Comparable Product	
SPECIALIZED PRODUCTS	DAS1 Brush 'n Blend (Extender)	8001 Acry Blend	947 Extender	
	DAS10 Fabric Painting Medium	300 Textile Medium	794 Fabric Medium	
	DAS11 Control Medium (Thickner)		948 Thickner	

DecoArt™

Box 360, Stanford, KY 40484 (606)365-3193 Toll-Free (800)367-3047 Fax (606)365-9739

SPRING TIME HOME

Be sure to put several coats of varnish on any birdhouse you use outside for protection.

Side

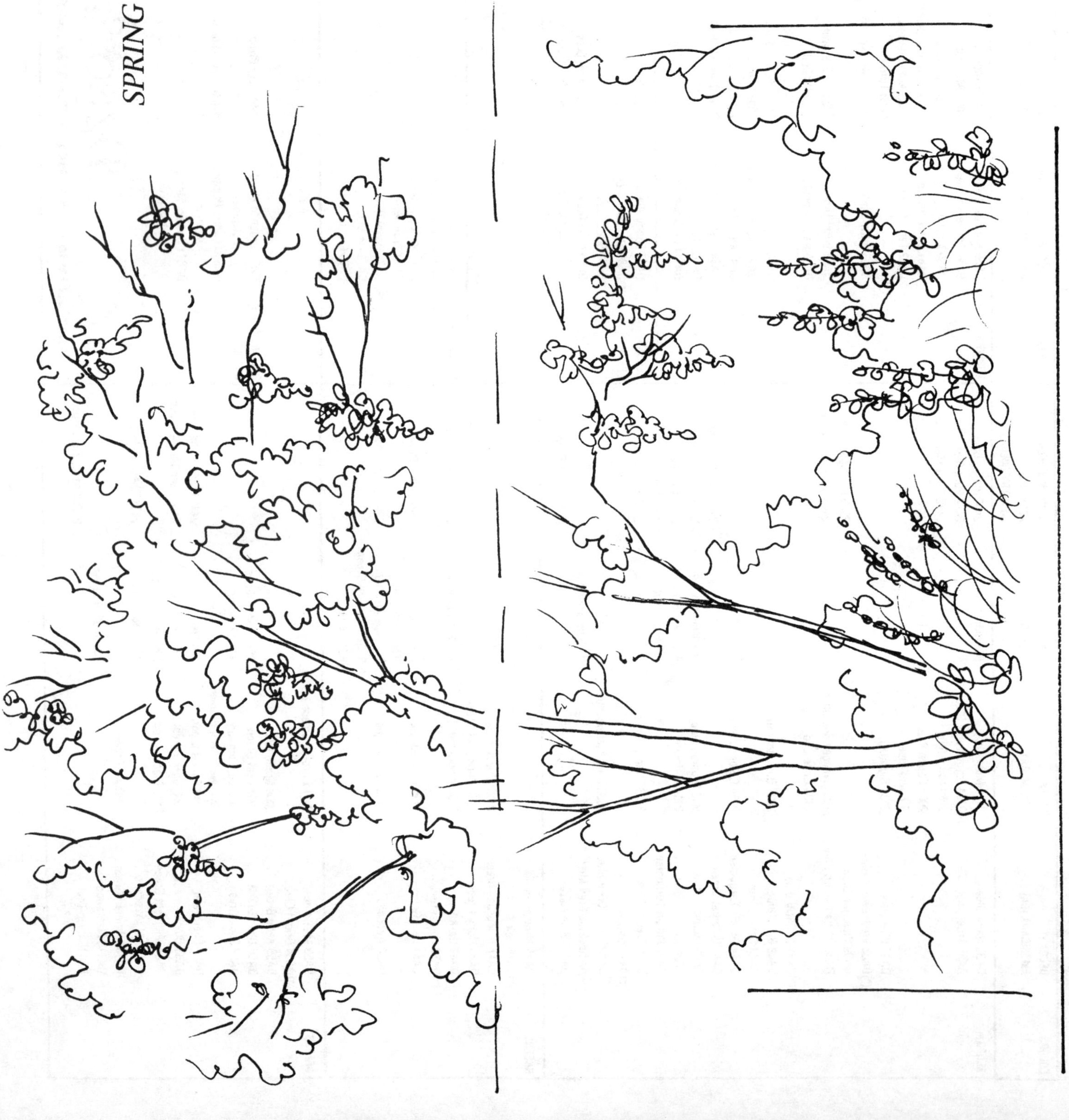

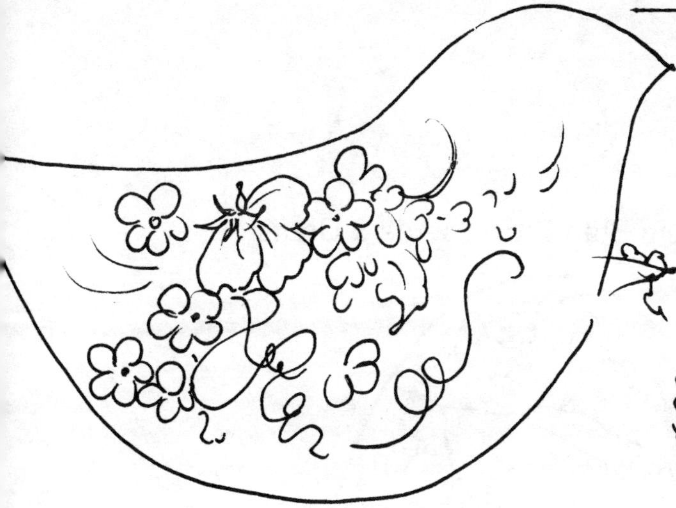

Side

Front

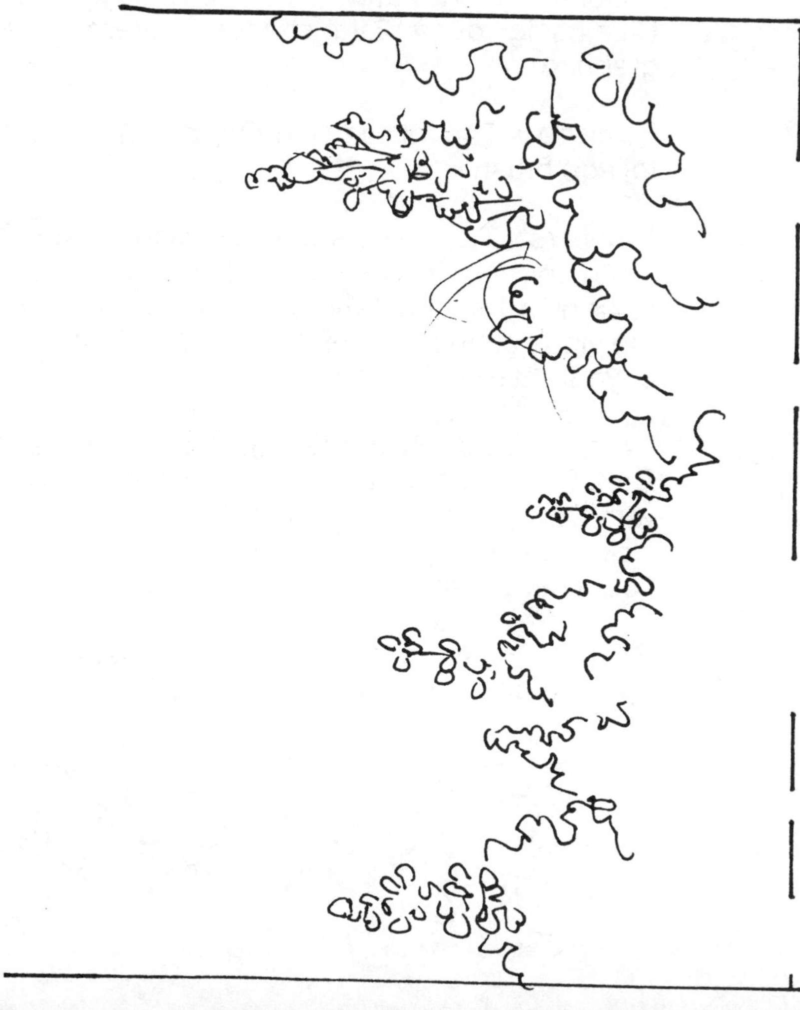

Back

© RBS 1994

Spring Time Home

Surface:

Large Cloud Cabin - and stand available from Stan Brown's Arts & Crafts

Palette: (Deco Americana Acrylic)

Titanium White
Avocado
Olive Green
Evergreen
Dark Chocolate
Burgundy Wine
Baby Blue
Sapphire
Dioxazine Purple
Cad. Yellow

Brushes:

#6 Round Brush
#4 Filbert Brush
#1 Liner Brush
#12 Flat Shader
Susie's Foliage Brush

Basecoat & Pattern: Basecoat birdhouse and stand with White Lightning. Allow to dry and sand lightly. Paint roof with Evergreen and trim roof and bottom edge with Baby Blue. Paint suggestion of shingles on roof with Baby Blue using your #12 flat shader. Pattern flowers and foliage shapes with gray graphite.

Foliage: Tap foliage with Evergreen, Avocado and Olive green using your foliage brush.

Flowers: Tap flowers with Burgundy Wine, Dioxazine Purple and Sapphire using your # 6 round brush. Highlight and form little flowers on top with base color plus Titanium White. Tap a few extra leaves in the tree on the roof and the vines on the front of the house with Avocado and Olive Green using the tip of your #6 round.

Tree Trunks, Branches and Grass: Paint tree trunks and branches with Dark Chocolate using your liner brush. Highlight these trunks and branches with Dark Chocolate and Titanium White. Paint grass with Olive Green by flicking up with your liner brush. Add a few stems and dots with Avocado using your liner brush.

Stand: Paint the stand in a similar manner. I wanted it to look as if vines were growing up the stand.

Sunflower Garden Set

Surface:
Trowel, Gardening Gloves Straw Hat, and Flower Pot

Palette: (Deco Americana Acrylic)
Titanium White
Avocado
Olive Green
Evergreen
Cad. Yellow
Cad Orange
Dark Chocolate
Antique Gold

Brushes:
#4 and 8 Filbert Brush
1/2 inch Angle Shader
Susie's Foliage Brush
#1 Liner Brush

Basecoat: Refer to general direction as to basecoat on flower pot, trowels, and patterning on straw hats.

Foliage: Tap foliage on to surface with Evergreen, Avocado and Olive Green using Susie's' Foliage Brush. Allow to dry.

Pattern: Pattern Sunflowers and filler flowers as desired with white graphite.

Sunflowers: Paint Sunflower petals Antique Gold using filbert brush (use the #4 or #8 filbert brush to suit the size of your sunflower), starting from the center of the flower and pulling to the outer tip of the petal. Tap centers with Dark Chocolate and shade with Cad. Yellow with a touch of Cad Orange . Highlight petals with Cad Yellow and Titanium White. Let some of the Antique Gold show through on the petals.

Leaves: Paint diamond shaped leaves with Evergreen and Avocado using your 1/2 inch angle shader. Highlight leaves with Olive Green.

Stems: Paint stems and squiggles with Avocado using you liner brush and a little water.

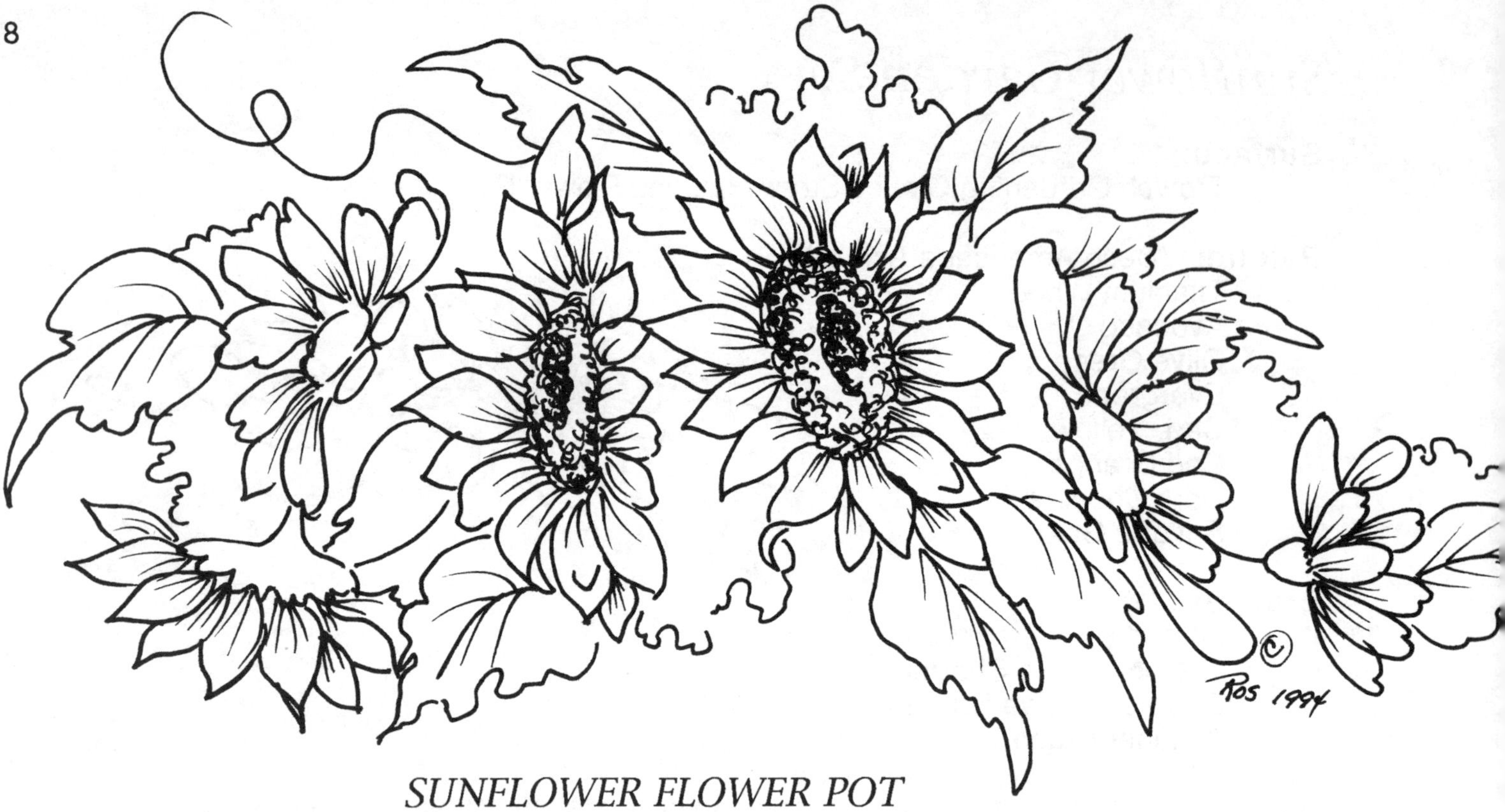

Ros 1994

SUNFLOWER FLOWER POT

What a wonderful gift to paint for special people that seem to have everthing and are hard to buy a gift for.

Ros 1994

SUNFLOWER HAT

BASE PETALS WITH ANTIQUE GOLD.

ADD MORE PETALS ON TOP.
CAD. YELLOW

PETALS WITH CAD. YELLOW + WHITE

TAP CENTERS WITH DARK CHOCOLATE.
HIGHLIGHT WITH CAD. YELLOW + CAD. ORANGE

SUNFLOWERS

BRUSH - FILBERT - CHISEL CORNER

Imagine, you could create a summer garden party with placemats and napkins adorned with fresh painted daisys.

Paint a canvas tote bag for each guest to take home, guarantee that they will cherish it.

SUNFLOWER GLOVES

BASE - MAGENTA

HIGHLIGHT PETALS - LOAD WITH MAGENTA - TIP WITH HIGHLIGHT COLORS

BASE CENTER WITH GREEN OLIVE AND TULIP YELLOW

SHADE WITH VIOLET DOTS - VIOLET

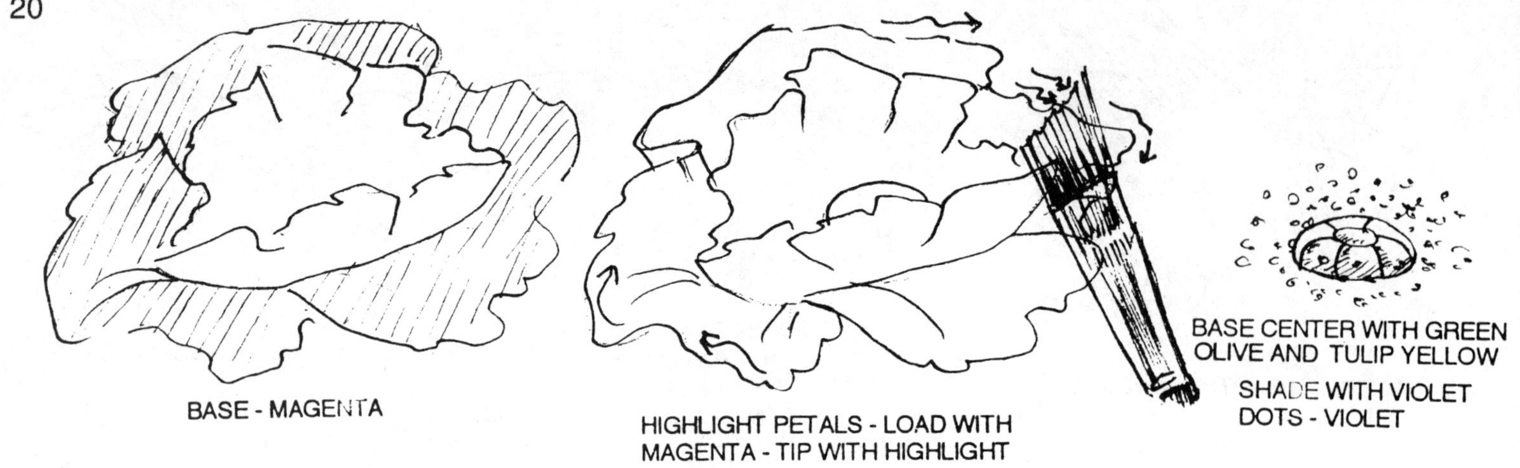

POPPY FLOWERS

POPPIES

BRUSH - 3/8 INCH ANGLE SHADER

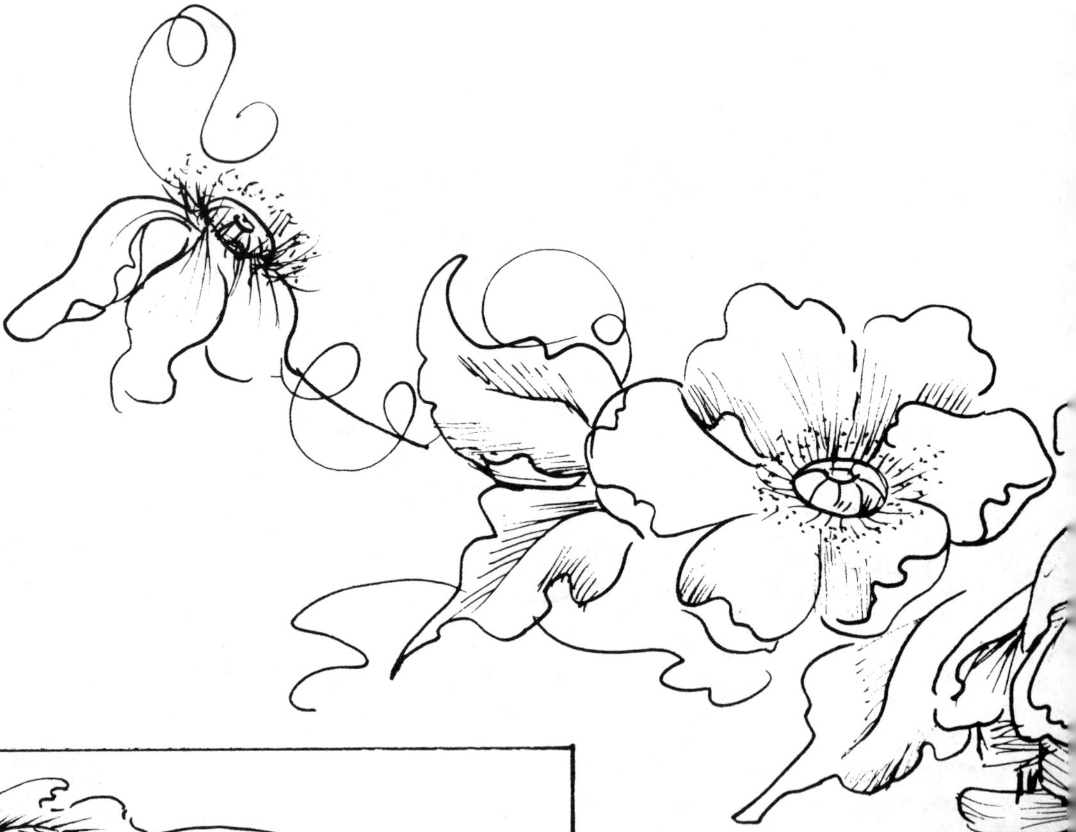

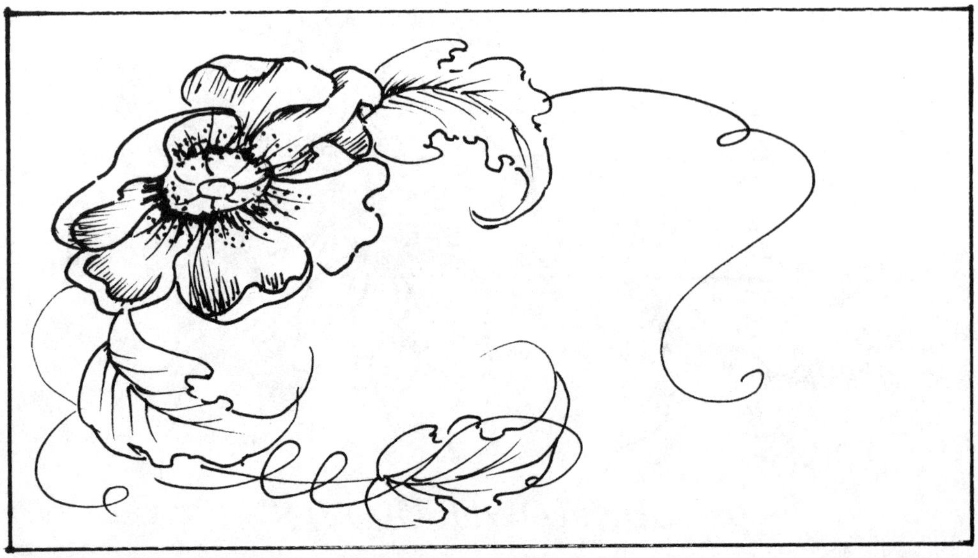

BASKET OF POPPIES

Basket of Poppies

Surface:
White Knit Shirt

Palette: (Grumbacher fabric dyes)
Comet Blue
Magenta
India Green
Green Olive
Violet
Super Hide White
Textile Medium

Brushes:
#4 Filbert Brush
3/8" Angle Shader
#1 Liner Brush
.05 Pigma Pen

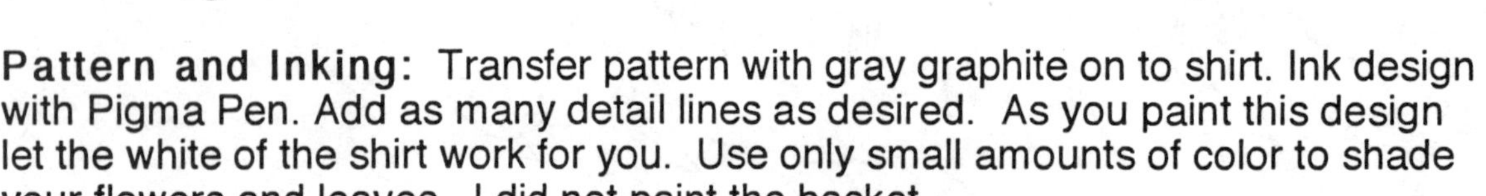

Pattern and Inking: Transfer pattern with gray graphite on to shirt. Ink design with Pigma Pen. Add as many detail lines as desired. As you paint this design let the white of the shirt work for you. Use only small amounts of color to shade your flowers and leaves. I did not paint the basket.

Poppies: Paint poppies one petal at a time with textile medium using your angle shader. Paint each petal while still wet using a small amount of Magenta on the point of the angle shader. Place color next to center of flower and pull streaks with the edge of your brush. Shade with a little Magenta and Violet near the center of the flower and separate between the petals. Keep most of the petals the white of the shirt, add Super Hide White as needed. Tint some flowers pink and some Violet and Comet Blue Paint flower centers with India green and shade with a little Green Olive. Paint Violet dots around the centers with the tip of the Liner Brush.

Leaves: Paint leaves on at a time with textile medium, while still wet paint a small amount of India Green or Green Olive down the vein of the leaf and on the opposite edge. Shade the leaves with a touch of Violet. Allow to dry.

Background Tint: Moisten the background areas around the flowers and leaves with textile medium. Paint small touches of greens and blue on damp surface using a little water in your paint to keep colors light and washed out.

Bow: Moisten bow, one loop at a time, with textile medium. Shade bow with small amount of Violet and Comet Blue. Highlight the bow with Super Hide White.

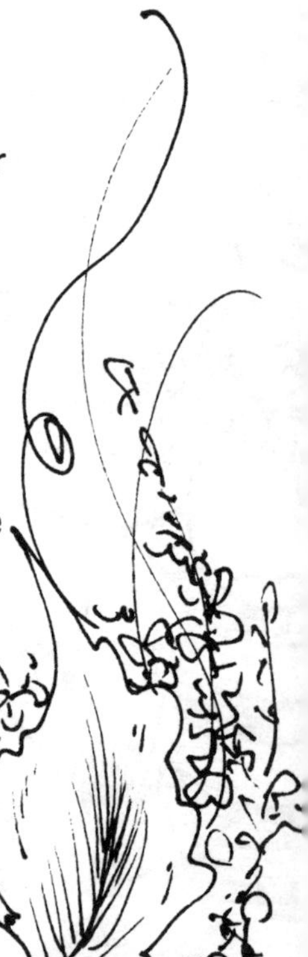

Grape Basket and Grape Tote Box

Use the Grape Tote Box to fill with napkins, silverware, flowers or as the centerpiece for a wine tasting party.

Surface:
Cooler Basket and Wood Tote Box

Palette: (Deco Americana Acrylic)
Titanium White
Dioxazine Purple
Orchid
Boysenberry Pink
True Blue
Burgundy wine
Dark Chocolate
Mint Julep
Olive green
Avocado
Baby Blue
Evergreen

Brushes:
1/4 inch and 3/8 inch Angle Shader
Susie's Foliage Brush
#1 Liner Brush
#12 Flat Shader

Basecoat: Base entire basket with white lightning, sand lightly. Paint the top of basket with Evergreen, allow to dry.

Pattern: Pattern as much as you feel you need, main lines of grapes and leaves.

Leaves: Using #12 flat shader highlight the edges and center vein of the leaves using Olive Green, Mint Julep, Avocado. Let the dark green background color be the base color for your leaves (see color illustration). Accent with True Blue, and Burgundy wine. Do not be afraid to add and loose leaves to suit you.

Grapes: Base grapes with Dioxazine Purple and True Blue using 3/8 inch angle shade, corner load 1/4 inch angle shader and highlight on left side with Orchid and Boysenberry Pink. Shade on right side with True blue and touches of Baby blue. Add strong white highlight for shine on left side (see illustration).

Foliage: Tap some foliage over the edges with foliage brush Using Evergreen, Avocado Green and Olive Green.

Stems: Paint stems with Dark Chocolate using your liner brush and a little water to make the paint fluid. Highlight these stems on the top with Dark Chocolate and Titanium White. Paint tendricles with Olive Green.

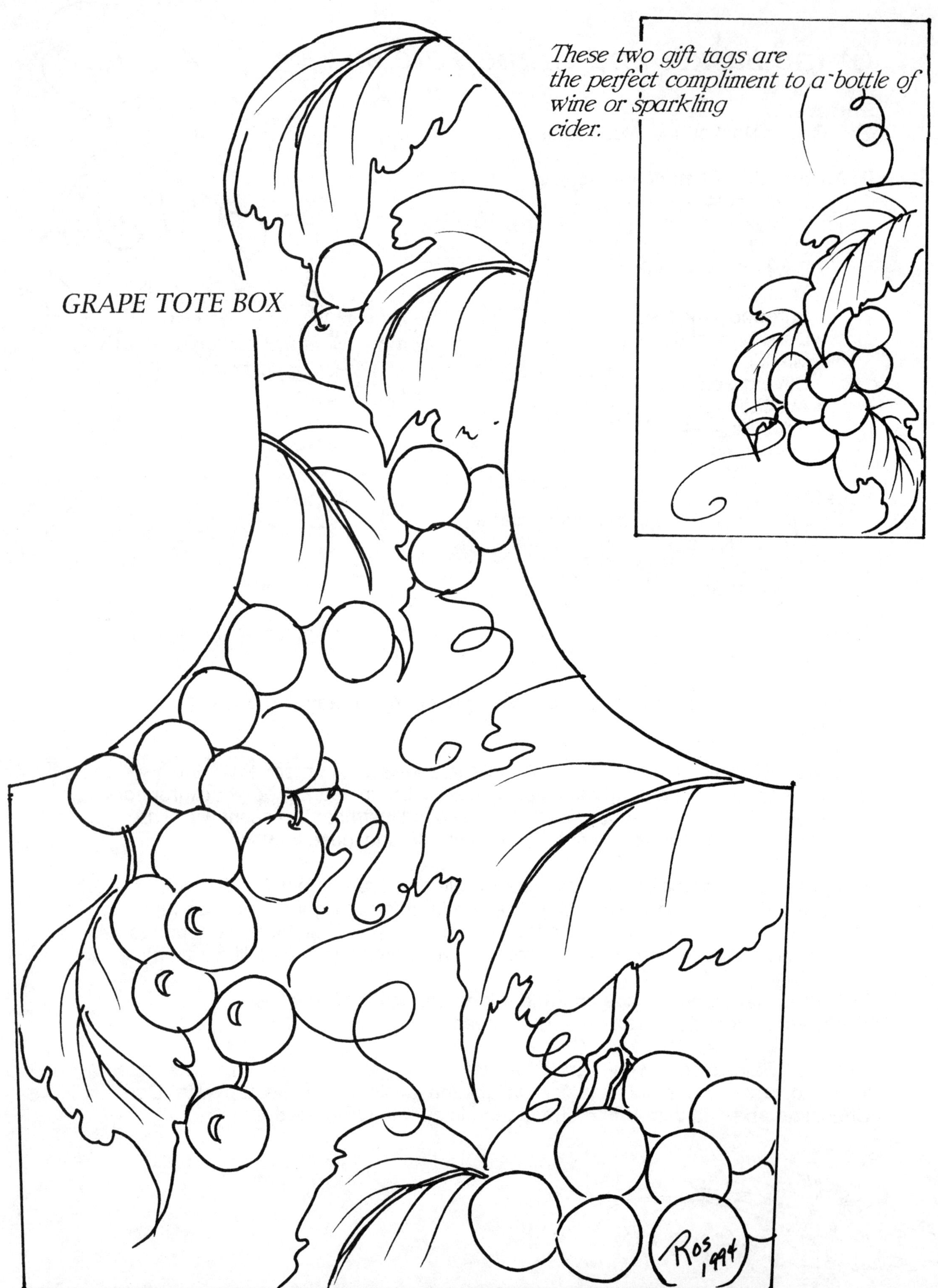
These two gift tags are the perfect compliment to a bottle of wine or sparkling cider.
GRAPE TOTE BOX
Ros 1994

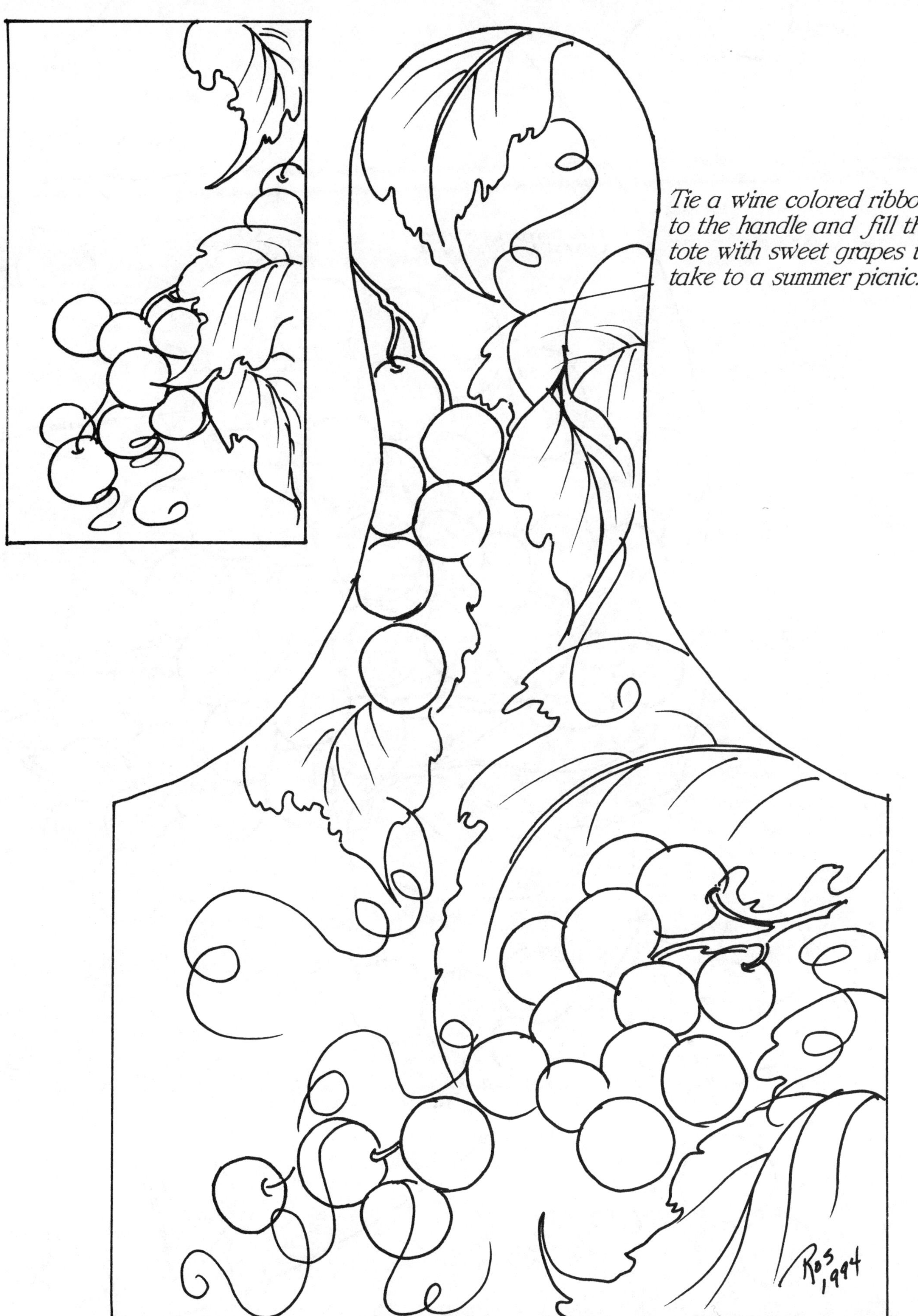

Tie a wine colored ribbon to the handle and fill the tote with sweet grapes to take to a summer picnic.

GRAPE BASKET

Ros 1994
This design would also be lovely on a wooden plate, remember though, to protect yourself and the surface by placing a glass on top.
A bentwood box be beautiful as well.

This little bench is the perfect size for that Angel Baby. What a fabulous keepsake to treasure for years to come.

Angel Baby Bench

Surface:
Wood Bench
Stan Brown's Arts & Crafts

Palette: (Deco Americana Acrylic)
Titanium White
Avocado
Olive Green
Dark Chocolate
Brandy Wine
Cad Orange
Sapphire
Antique Gold
Raw Sienna
Cad. Yellow

Brushes:
#6 Round Brush
#4 Filbert Brush
#1 Liner Brush
1/4 inch and 3/8 inch Angle Shader

Basecoat & Pattern: Basecoat bench with White Lightning. Allow to dry and sand lightly. Pattern Angel and flowers with gray graphite. This is my little Angel, she is 8 months old and I traced a photograph of her, added more hair and angel wings. This bench will end up in her room I am sure, hope she will love it when she has an Angel Baby of her own.

Angel Baby: Take your time with this little angel. Paint all her skin excert her eyes with a mixture of Titanium White, touch of Dark Chocolate and touch of Brandy Wine (mix a little puddle of flesh color), use your 1/4 inch angle shader. Look at the photograph carefully. Shade her face with flesh color and a little Dark Chocolate on the tip of your 1/4 inch angle shader. Highlight her forehead, nose, chin, and cheeks with Titanium White. Add a touch of Pink to her cheeks and lips with flesh color and touch of Brandy Wine and Cad. Orange. Paint her hair with Raw Sienna and shade darker at the top of her head with Dark Chocolate. Paint curls with a mixture of Antique Gold and Titanium White using your liner brush. My Angle Baby has dark eyes so I painted them with Dark Chocolate. Highlight with small white dot. Paint eyebrows and lashes with Raw Sienna and a little Dark Chocolate using your liner brush. Keep these light and delicate. Paint wings with Titanium White and shade with a gray made with Dark Chocolate, Sapphire, and Titanium White. Paint a suggestion of fabric drape with Titanium White using your angle shader.

Flowers: Tap little flowers with Sapphire, Brandy Wine, and Titanium White using your #6 round brush. Form little flower petals on top with base color and Titanium White. Paint Daisies with Titanium White using #4 filbert brush. Paint

I took one of the many photos from our special Angel Grandbaby and used it for a model. You may want to paint your own angel babies face. If you are not up to painting a face, then just add a few more flowers to the design.

I used this same design as a border around the little lamp and watering can. You might think of other ways to apply this border design to furniture or cupboards.

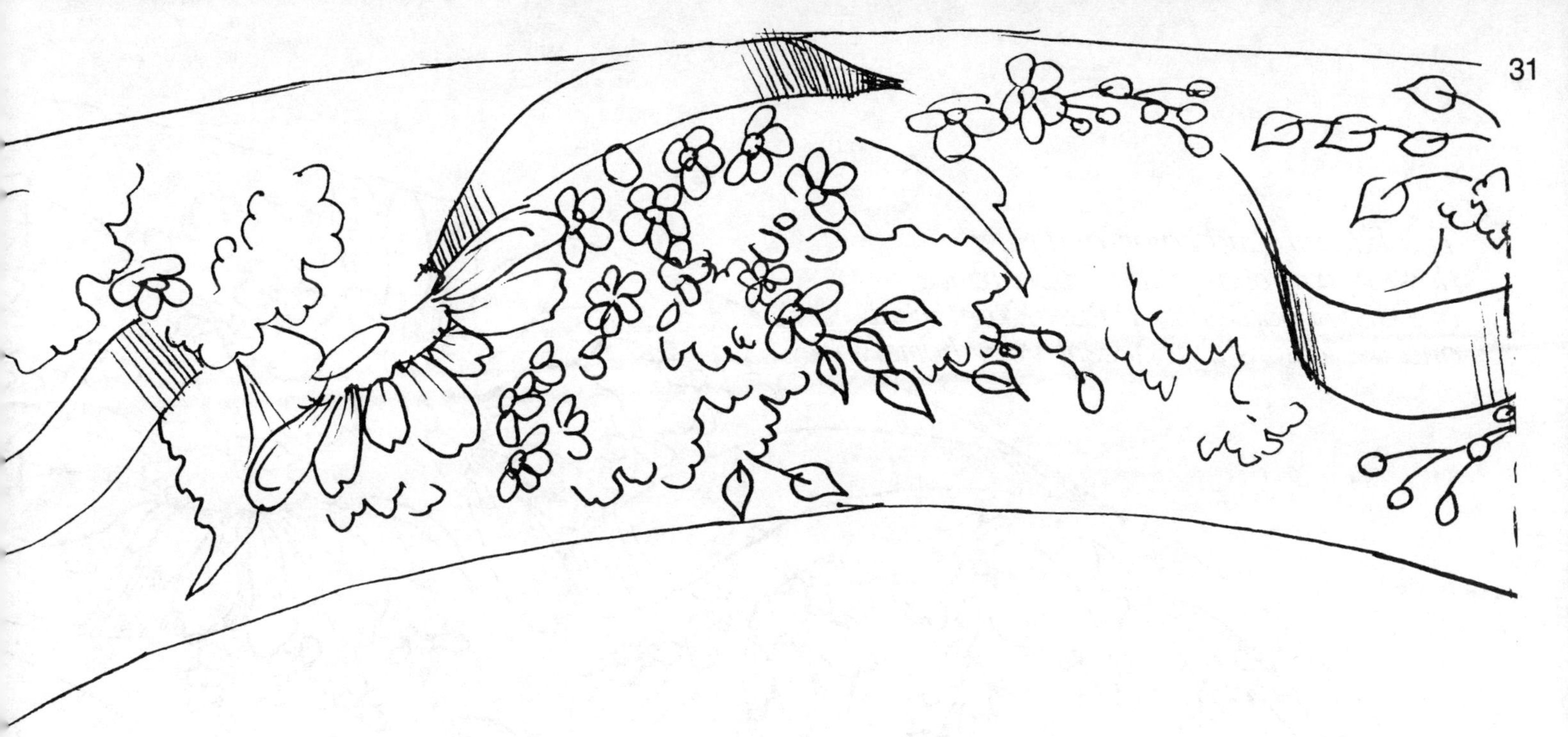

DAISY DOODLES & DABS

Cut a placemat from canvas and use as a table centerpiece. Apply an extra coat of gesso and a couple coats of varnish for protection.

The background color, and filler flowers can change the appearance of Daisy Doodles & Dabs. Experiment and use colors that accent your home.

Daisy Doodles & Dabs

Surface:
Cooler basket or oval wooden frame.

Palette:
White
Olive Green
Avocado
Evergreen
Cad. Yellow
Dark Chocolate
Baby Blue
True Blue
Boysenberry Pink
Burgundy Wine
Lavender
Dioxazine Purple

Brushes:
Susie's Foliage Brush
#4 & 8 Filbert Brush
#1 Liner Brush
3/8" Angle Shader
#20 Flat Shader

DAISY CROCK LID

Basecoat: Basecoat basket or mirror with White Lightning. After basket is dry sand lightly.

Foliage: Tap background foliage with all shades of green using your foliage brush starting with the Evergreen and tapping your brush into Olive Green, Baby Blue, and Avocado. Allow to dry.

Daisies: Pattern daisies and filler flowers as needed with white graphite. Paint the daisy petals and centers with Titanium White using #8 filbert brush. Paint daisy centers with Cad Yellow, shade with Dark Chocolate and touch of Burgundy Wine (see daisy illustration).

Filler Flowers: Paint filler flowers with # 4 filbert brush. Tap with tip of brush, clusters of flowers using Dioxazine Purple and Dioxazine Purple /True Blue. While still wet add taps of Lavender, True Blue, Baby Blue, and Titanium White, forming little flower shapes by placing three or four taps together, vary colors and keep shapes loose and airy. Add Cad Yellow dots for centers of these little flowers.

Ribbon: Paint the basket ribbon with Boysenberry Pink and Titanium White using your angle shader (Load brush with Boysenberry Pink and corner load with Titanium White). Paint the ribbon on the mirror frame ribbon with Baby Blue and Titanium White.

Stems, Squiggles, & Leaves: Add squiggles with Olive Green and Avocado using your liner brush. Paint little stems on filler flowers with Avocado using your liner brush. Paint extra leaves with Avocado and Evergreen using your angle shader

DELPHINIUM RECIPE BOX

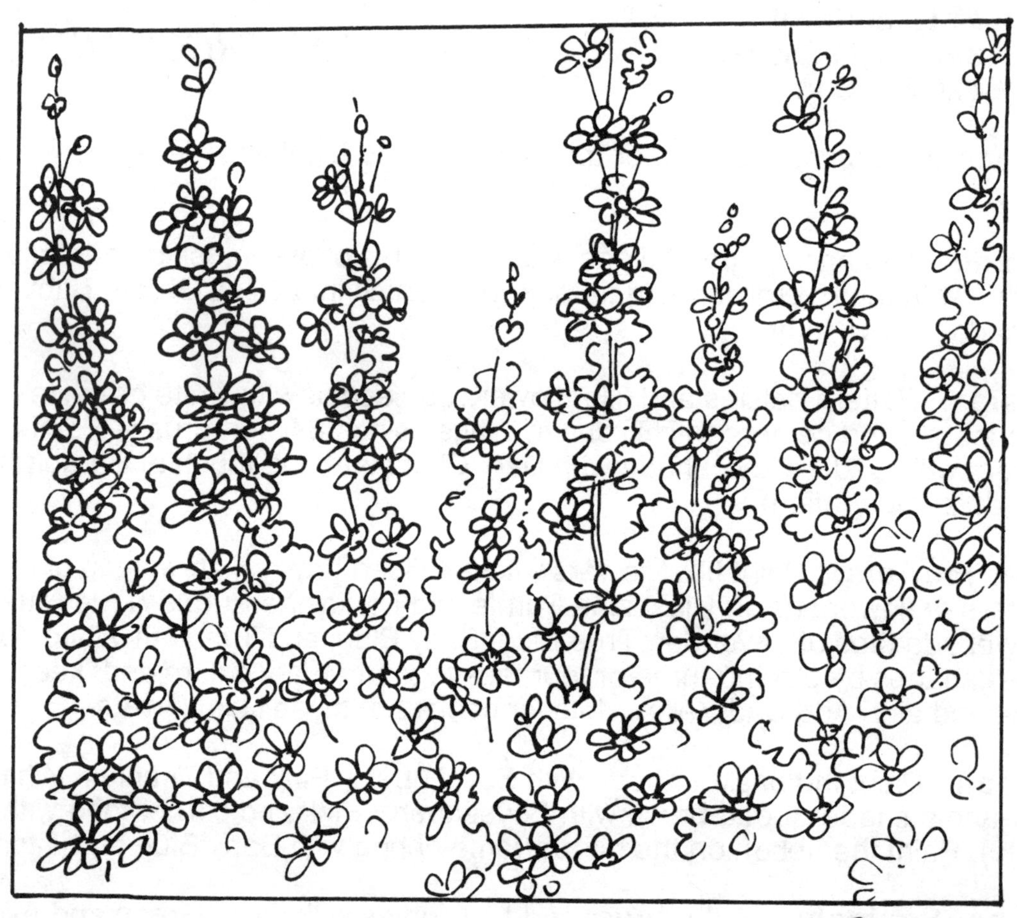

Delphiniums

Surface:
Recipe box and crock lid

Palette: (Deco Americana Acrylic)
Titanium White
Olive Green
Evergreen
Lavender
Cad. Yellow
Burgundy Wine
Boysenberry Pink
True Blue
Dioxazine Purple

Brushes:
#6 Round Brush
#12 Flat Shader
#1 Liner Brush

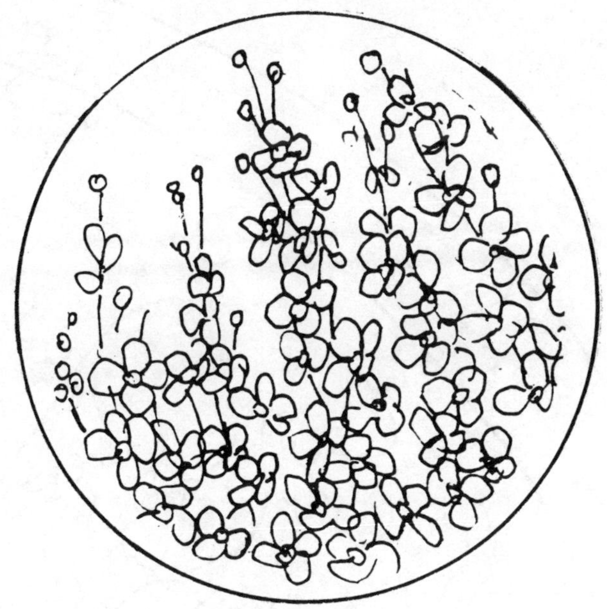

DELIPHINIUM CROCK LID

Basecoat: Paint two coats of White Lightning on recipe box and sand lightly. Mask the center of the box with 1" masking tape. Paint the center area with one coat of Evergreen. The color is transparent and the wood grain will show through. Paint the rim on the box top and lower edge with Evergreen.

Delphiniums: Pattern the delphiniums and ribbon with graphite if desired. Refer to flower worksheet for delphinium structure. Base each flower with either Burgundy Wine, Olive Green, or Dioxazine Purple and True Blue,using the tip of #6 round brush. Tap little flower petal on top of each clump with base color plus Titanium White using tip of #6 round.

Stems: Paint little stems with Olive Green using your liner brush and a little water. Add little Cad. Yellow dots for flower centers and Titanium White dots for buds.

Ribbon: Paint the ribbon with Boysenberry Pink using your #12 flat shader. Shade with Burgundy Wine and a little Dioxazine Purple. Highlight the ribbon with Titanium White.

Trim: Edge box and around the center square with a mix of Lavender and Burgundy Wine using your liner brush and a little water.

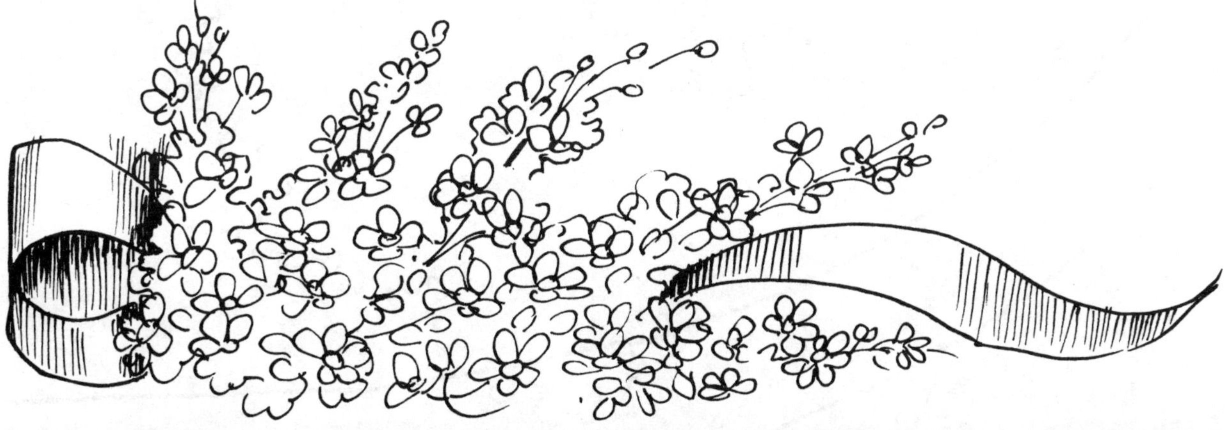

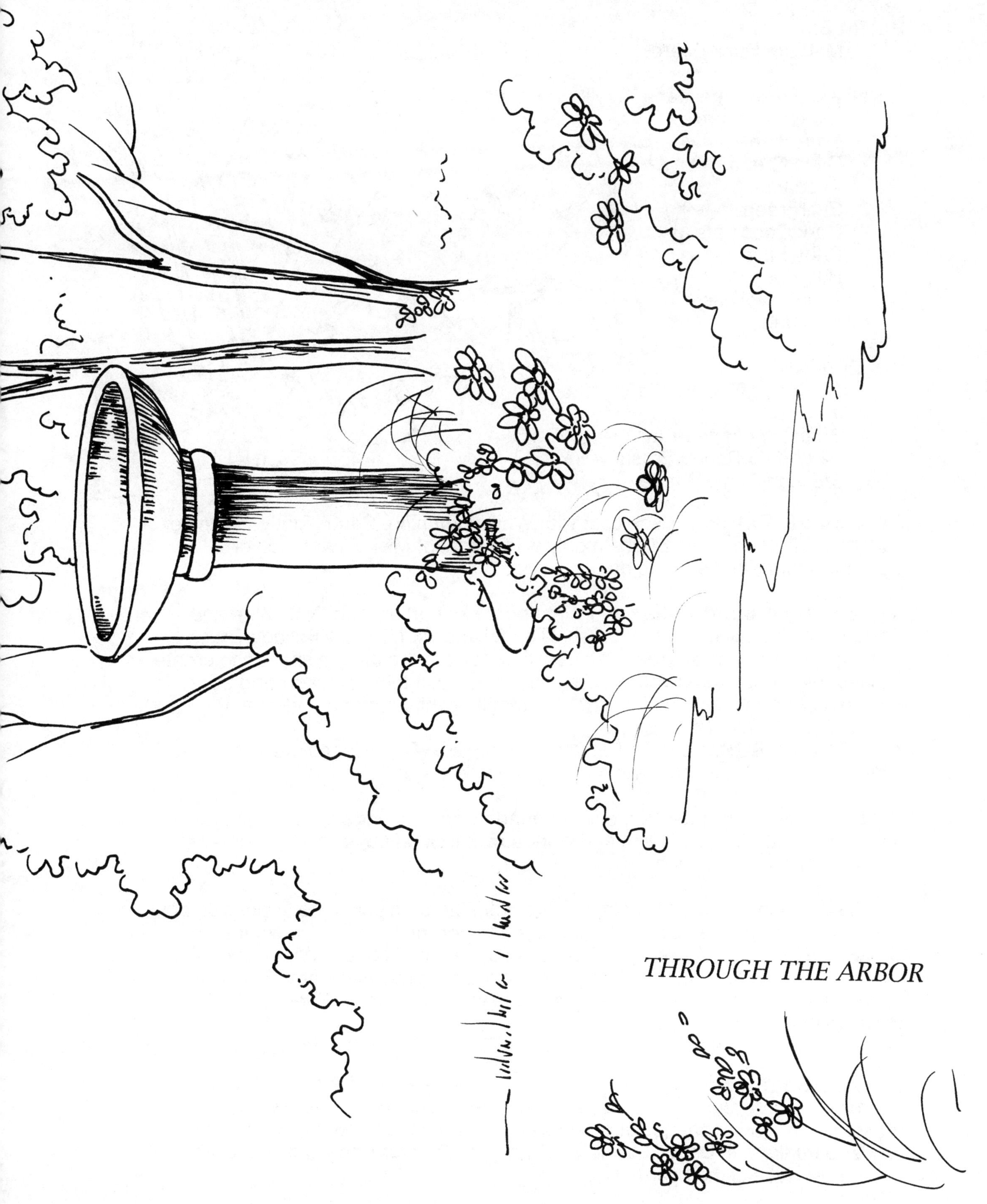

THROUGH THE ARBOR

Through The Arbor

Surface:
Medium Duck Board

Palette: (Deco Americana Acrylic)
Dioxazine Purple
True Blue
Olive Green
Avocado
Evergreen
Dark Chocolate
Baby Blue
Burgundy Wine
Titanium White
Mint Julep

Brushes:
#12 Flat Synthetic
I Liner
Susie's Foliage Brush
#2 and #6 Round Brush
3/8 inch Angle Shader

Basecoat & Pattern: Base coat with White Lightning. Sand lightly. Transfer pattern of birdbath. Paint Birdbath only with a coat of Misket (water color blocking agent), and allow to dry.

Sky & Background Foliage: Paint upper sky portion with Baby blue and Titanium White using #20 Flat brush. Tap foliage with Susie's Foliage Brush starting with the lightest greens and building toward the middle shades to create bushes and trees. Keep your colors soft and hazy in these background trees. Paint over birdbath as the Misket will protect the white surface underneath.

Tree Trunks & Branches: Paint tree trunks with Dark Chocolate and a little Titanium White using your liner brush and a little water.

Grass: Flick up for grass in the foreground using side edge of your foliage brush. Start at the ground line and work down, flicking up, using light greens and Titanium White.

Birdbath: Allow to dry. Remove Misket from birdbath using the sticky side of a piece of masking tape. Shade the Birdbath under the bowl and down the right side with a mixture of True Blue, Dark Chocolate,and Titanium White using the corner of your angle shader. Paint water in the birdbath with Baby Blue and Titanium White, shade the lower edge of the water with True Blue and Dark Chocolate.

Edge of Board: Paint lattice effect on the outside edge of the board with Evergreen using your #12 flat brush. Tap foreground trees, bushes and grasses with darker shades of green using your foliage brush. Add branches and tree trunks with Dark Chocolate. Paint some darker trees and branches on the front surface of the board.

#1
#2
#3
LIRIOPE
#1
#2
DELPHINIUMS
#1
#2
IMPATIENS
BASKET
FOLIAGE
& BRANCH

DAISY GARDEN SET
PAGES 74, 75, 76
MY GARDEN
Pages 64, 65

SPRING BASKET
Pages 56, 57

DAISY GLOVES
Pages 75

DAISY DOODLES & DABS
Pages 30, 31, 32, 33

ANGEL BABY BENCH
Pages 28, 29
BABY HAT
Page 75

DAISY DOODLES & DABS
Pages 72, 73

DASIY CROCK LID
Page 33

DAISY HAT
Page 74

DAISY
GRAPE
LEAVES
BLEND
ROSE
DARK
RIBBON

Flowers & Grasses: Paint flowers with Dioxazine Purple, Burgundy Wine, and Titanium White, using the tip of #6 round brush. Vary these flowers from dark to light to get different colors and styles as you would find in a garden. Paint fine line grasses and some squiggley vines with Olive green and Avocado using your liner brush and a little water. Refer to photograph for placement.

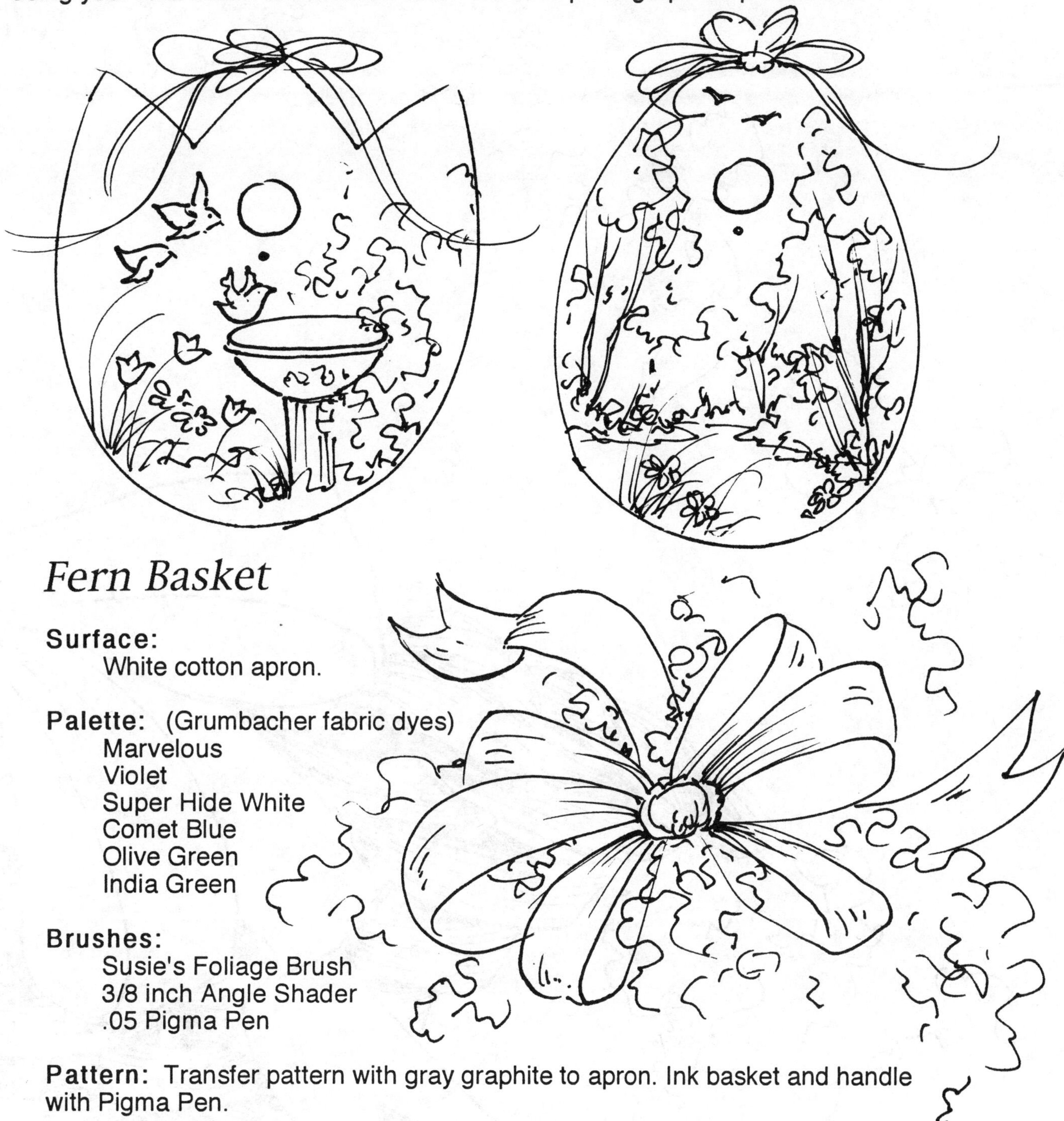

Fern Basket

Surface:
White cotton apron.

Palette: (Grumbacher fabric dyes)
Marvelous
Violet
Super Hide White
Comet Blue
Olive Green
India Green

Brushes:
Susie's Foliage Brush
3/8 inch Angle Shader
.05 Pigma Pen

Pattern: Transfer pattern with gray graphite to apron. Ink basket and handle with Pigma Pen.

Fern: Tap fern with Green Olive, India Green, and Comet Blue using Susie's Foliage Brush. Add a little water to your brush (tap excess out on paper towel) as you tap into various colors. Tap touches of Violet and Super Hide White for accent.

Bow: Paint ribbon with Super Hide White using 3/8 inch angle shader. Shade ribbon with Marvelous. Refer to color photograph for color placement.

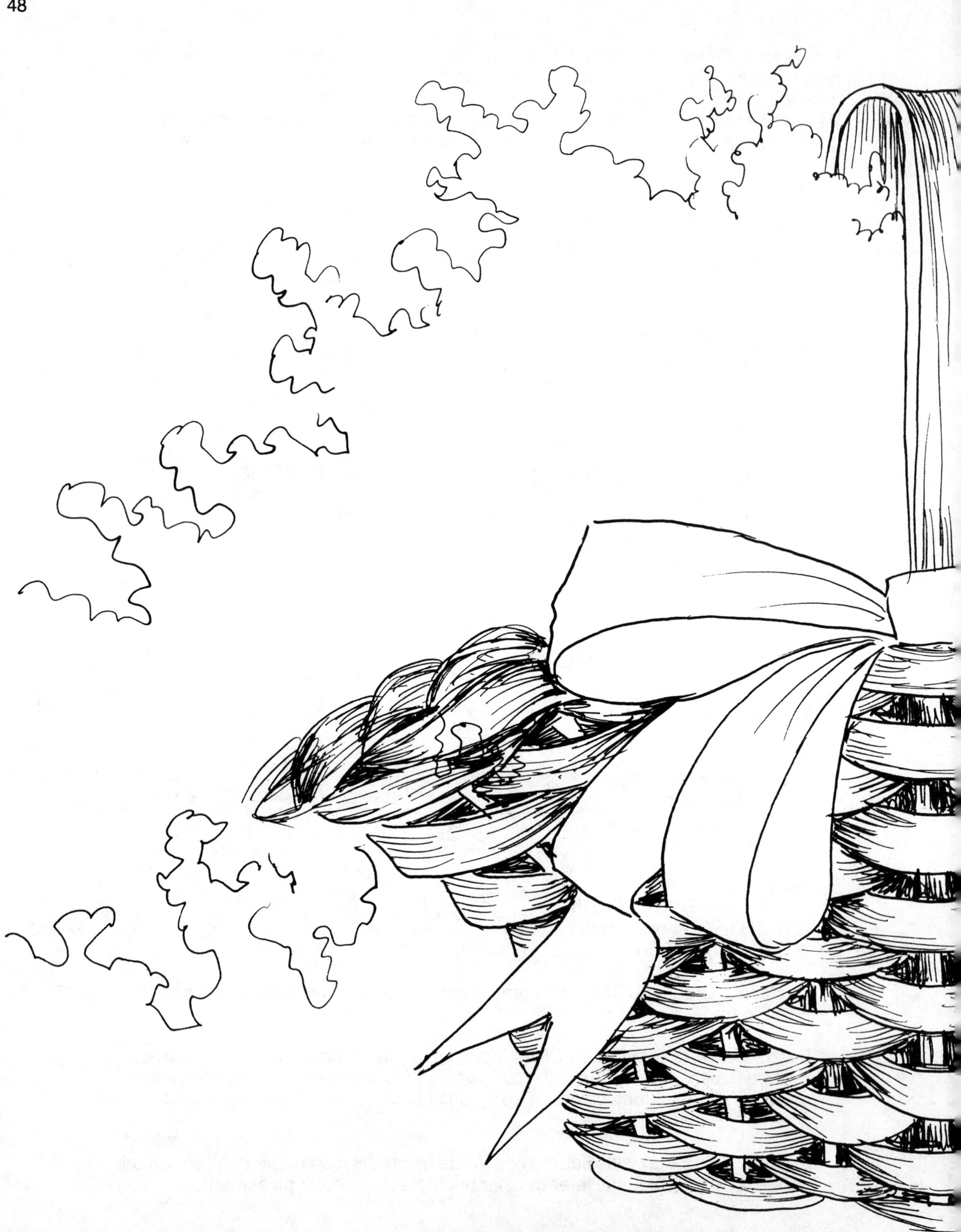

This is such a fun, easy design to paint and ink. You may want to put this on a wooden plaque for the yard with an inviting welcome. OR as a shower gift for the bride or mother to be.

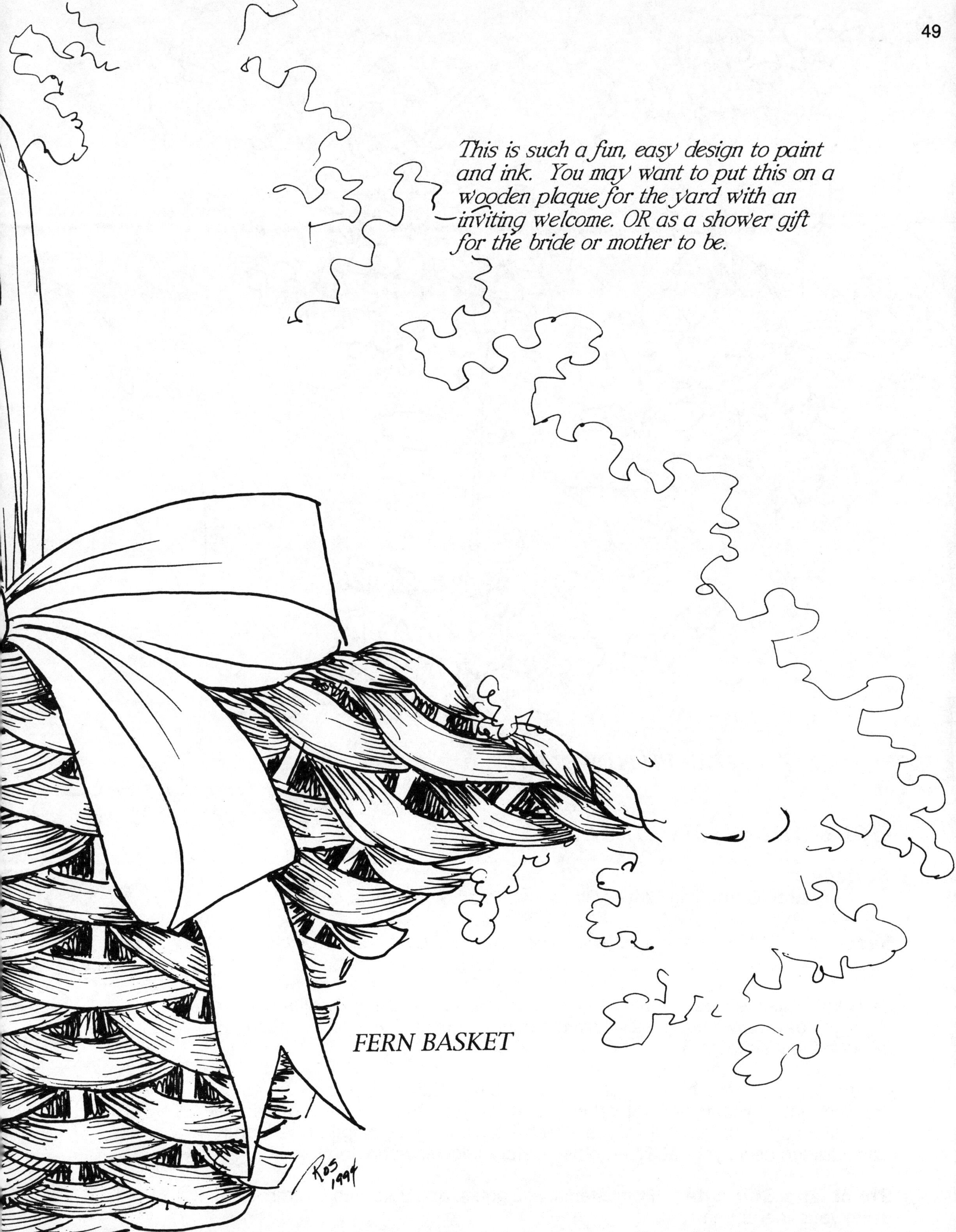

FERN BASKET

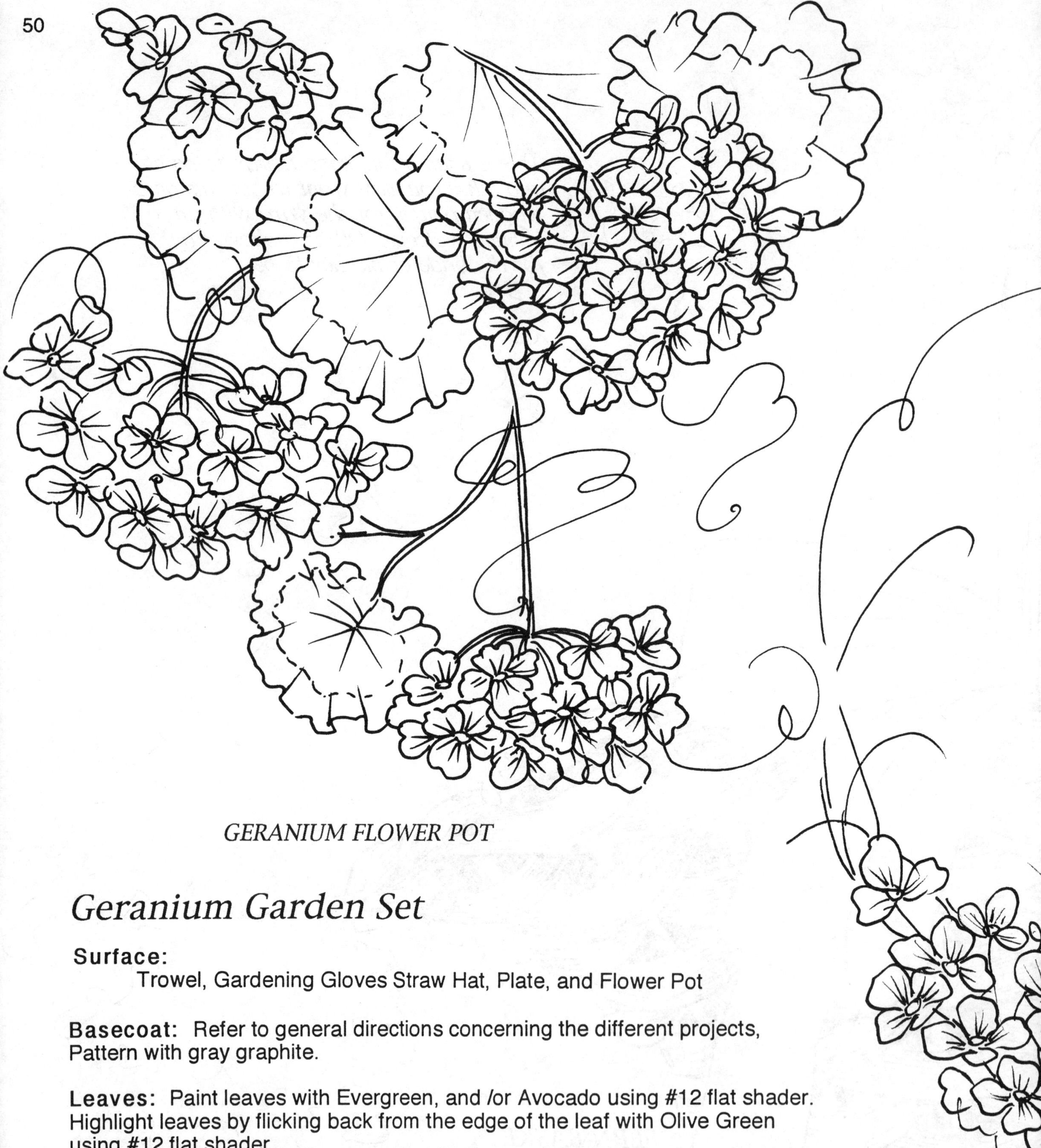

GERANIUM FLOWER POT

Geranium Garden Set

Surface:
Trowel, Gardening Gloves Straw Hat, Plate, and Flower Pot

Basecoat: Refer to general directions concerning the different projects, Pattern with gray graphite.

Leaves: Paint leaves with Evergreen, and /or Avocado using #12 flat shader. Highlight leaves by flicking back from the edge of the leaf with Olive Green using #12 flat shader.

Geraniums: Paint a base of color for flowers with Burgundy Wine using a dabbing motion with your #8 filbert brush. Keep you shape loose and irregular. Paint little petals on top of flower base with Titanium White, Napthol Red, and Cad. Orange using your #8 filbert brush (refer to flower worksheet).

Stems and Squiggles: Paint stems, squiggles, and dots with Evergreen using your liner brush.

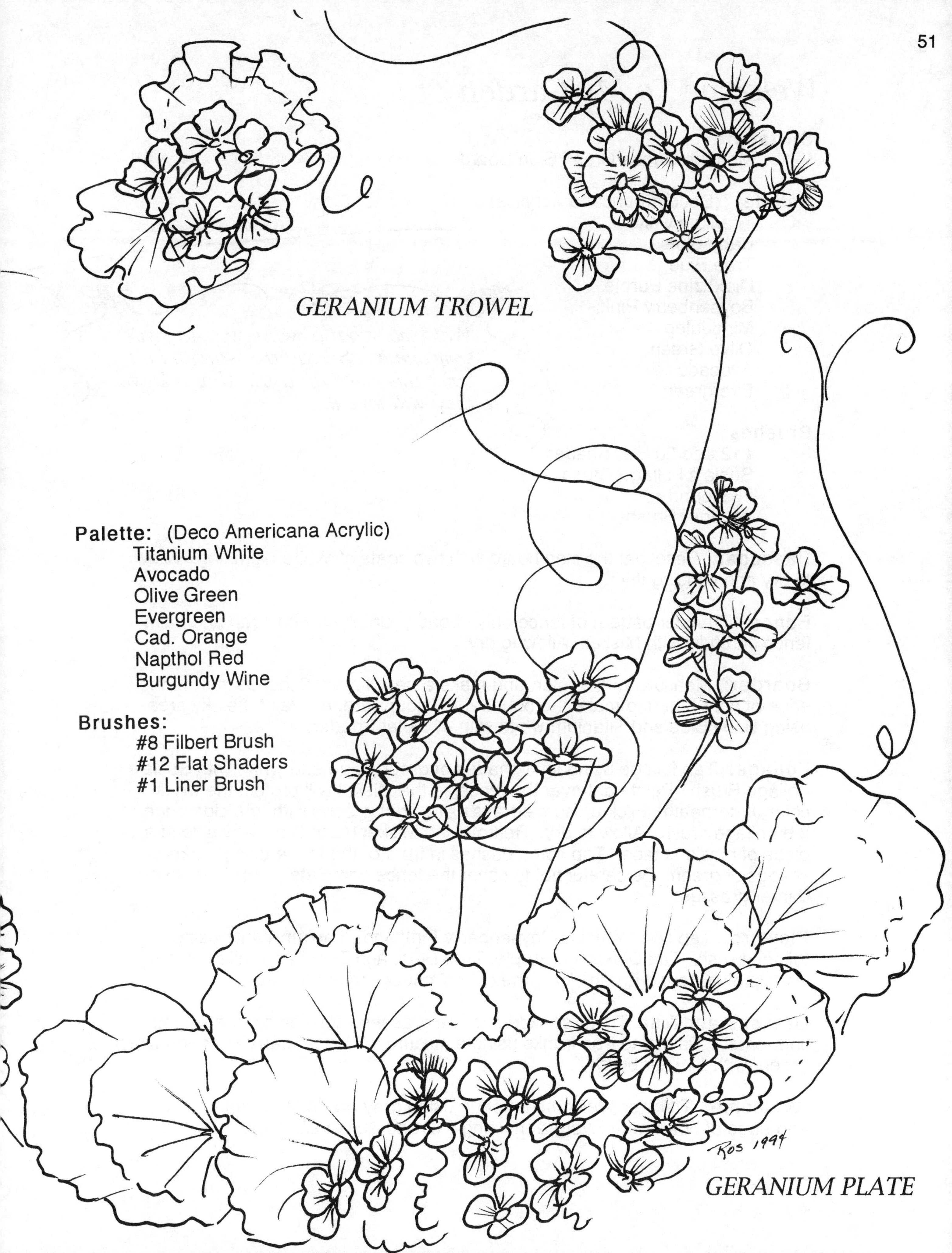

GERANIUM TROWEL

Palette: (Deco Americana Acrylic)
- Titanium White
- Avocado
- Olive Green
- Evergreen
- Cad. Orange
- Napthol Red
- Burgundy Wine

Brushes:
- #8 Filbert Brush
- #12 Flat Shaders
- #1 Liner Brush

GERANIUM PLATE

Welcome To My Garden

Surface:
Medium Goose Creek Sign Board

Palette: (Deco Americana Acrylics)
Titanium white
Baby Blue
True Blue
Dioxazine Purple
Boysenberry Pink
Mint Julep
Olive Green
Avocado
Evergreen

Welcome, what a warm way to invite someone in. Spread the warmth and paint this piece for a friend or relative, they will love it.

Brushes:
#12 and 20 Flat Shader
Susie's Foliage Brush
#6 Round
#1 Liner Brush

Basecoat: Basecoat the sign board with two coats of White Lightning. Allow to dry and sand lightly.

Fence: Transfer pattern of fence only. Load your brush with soap and paint fence carefully with Misket. Allow to dry.

Boarder: Measure with a ruler, and make a pencil mark 2 inches in from the edge of your board to make the boundary of your garden. Paint the sky area using Baby Blue and Titanium white with #20 Flat Shader.

Foliage: Tap foliage using light shades of green, blue and white with Susie's Foliage Brush. Paint right over the fence as the Misket will protect the white color underneath. Flick up some grass using light greens with the side edge of the Foliage brush. Allow to dry. Remove the Misket using the sticky side of a piece of masking tape. Tap some bushes in front of the fence using darker shades of green. Be careful not to cover the fence completely. Flick up some darker grasses.

Flowers: Tap flowers using Boysenberry Pink and Titanium White using foliage brush. Tap Dioxazine Purple, True Blue, and Titanium White flowers with tip of #6 round Brush. Vary the colors, check the photograph.

Grasses andTree Trunks: Add fine line grasses with Olive Green using #1 liner brush. Paint fine tree trunks using a mixture of Boysenberry Pink and Olive green. with #1 liner brush.

Welcome: Transfer *Welcome* lettering using gray graphite. Paint lettering and edge of board with Evergreen using #12 and 20 flat shaders.

Ros
1994

WELCOME TO MY GARDEN

Give a freind the gift of summer in full bloom year round. Hang the Welcome sign on a fence, a gate, a patio, or indoors. Be creative, paint the design onto your front door!

SURFACE
Stan Brown's Arts & Crafts

ome

Spring Basket

Surface:
Green cotton apron.

Palette: (Grumbacher fabric dyes)
Violet
Super Hide White
Peacock Blue
Green Olive
India Green
Light Brown
Dark Brown
Gold
Tulip Yellow
Dark Blue

Brushes:
Susie's Foliage Brush
12 Flat Shader
#1 Liner Brush
#4 and 8 Filbert Brush

Pattern: Transfer pattern of outline of basket and handle with white graphite to apron.

Basket: Base coat basket and handle with Light Brown using your #12 flat shader. Shade the edges and under the handle of the basket with Dark Brown. Paint basket weave with Gold and Super Hide White using the chisel edge of your #12 flat shader (refer to basket instructions).

Foliage: Tap filler foliage in the basket with Green Olive and India Green using Susie's Foliage Brush. Add a little water to your brush (tap excess out on paper towel) as you tap into various colors. Allow to dry.

Dasies: Pattern daises on top of foliage with white graphite. Paint centers with Tulip Yellow and shade with Light Brown using #8 filbert brush. Paint daisy petals with Super Hide White using #8 filbert brush (refer to daisy instructions).

Filler Flowers: Paint filler flowers with Violet and Dark Blue using #4 filbert brush. Add little petal flowers with Super Hide White, Violet, and Peacock Blue.

Stems: Paint little stems and squiggles with Olive Green and Super Hide White using your liner brush and a little water. Add some Super Hide White dots and Tulip Yellow flower centers with your liner brush.

A spring bouquet is the most cheerful way to chase away the winter blues and lighten up your heart.

SPRING BASKET

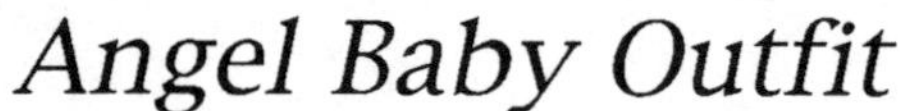

Angel Baby Outfit

Surface:
Overalls, Shirt, Shoes, Hat, and Bib

Palette: (Grumbacher Fabric Dye)
Super Hide White
Green Olive
Violet
Tulip Yellow
Light Brown
Violetta
Comet Blue
Magenta

Brushes:
#4 & 8 Filbert Brush
Susie's Foliage Brush
1/4" Angel Shader
#1 Liner Brush

Foliage: Tap foliage on to surface with Green Olive, Comet Blue, and Super Hide White using foliage brush. Keep foliage light and airy and allow to dry.

Pattern: Pattern Daisies and filler flowers as desired with white or gray graphite.

Flowers: Paint Daisy petals and centers with Super Hide White using #4 filbert brush. Paint centers with Tulip Yellow and shade with Light Brown. Tap filler flowers with Violet, Violetta and Comet Blue using your #6 round brush. Form little petals on top with Violetta and Super hide White and Comet Blue and Super Hide White.

Leaves: Paint little leaves with Green Olive using 1/4 inch angle shader. Highlight leaves with Comet Blue and Super Hide White.

Stems: Paint stems and squiggles with Green Olive and Super Hide White using you Liner Brush and a little water.

Ribbon: Paint ribbon on shirt to match overalls. I used Magenta, Super Hide White and a touch of Light Brown. Allow to dry a few minutes and paint Super Hide White stripes on ribbon with your liner brush.

centers with Cad. Yellow and shade with Dark Chocolate and a touch of Cad. Orange.

Leaves: Paint soft leaves with darker shades of green and a little water. Highlight with lighter shades of green using your angle shader. Paint some stems and squiggles with Olive Green and Avocado using your liner brush.

Ribbons: Paint ribbons with a soft shade made from Sapphire, Brandy Wine and Titanium White using your 3/8 inch angle shader. Highlight the ribbons with Titanium White to create satin effect. Shade the edges of the ribbon with Sapphire and Brandy Wine using the corner of your angle shader.

Ros
1994

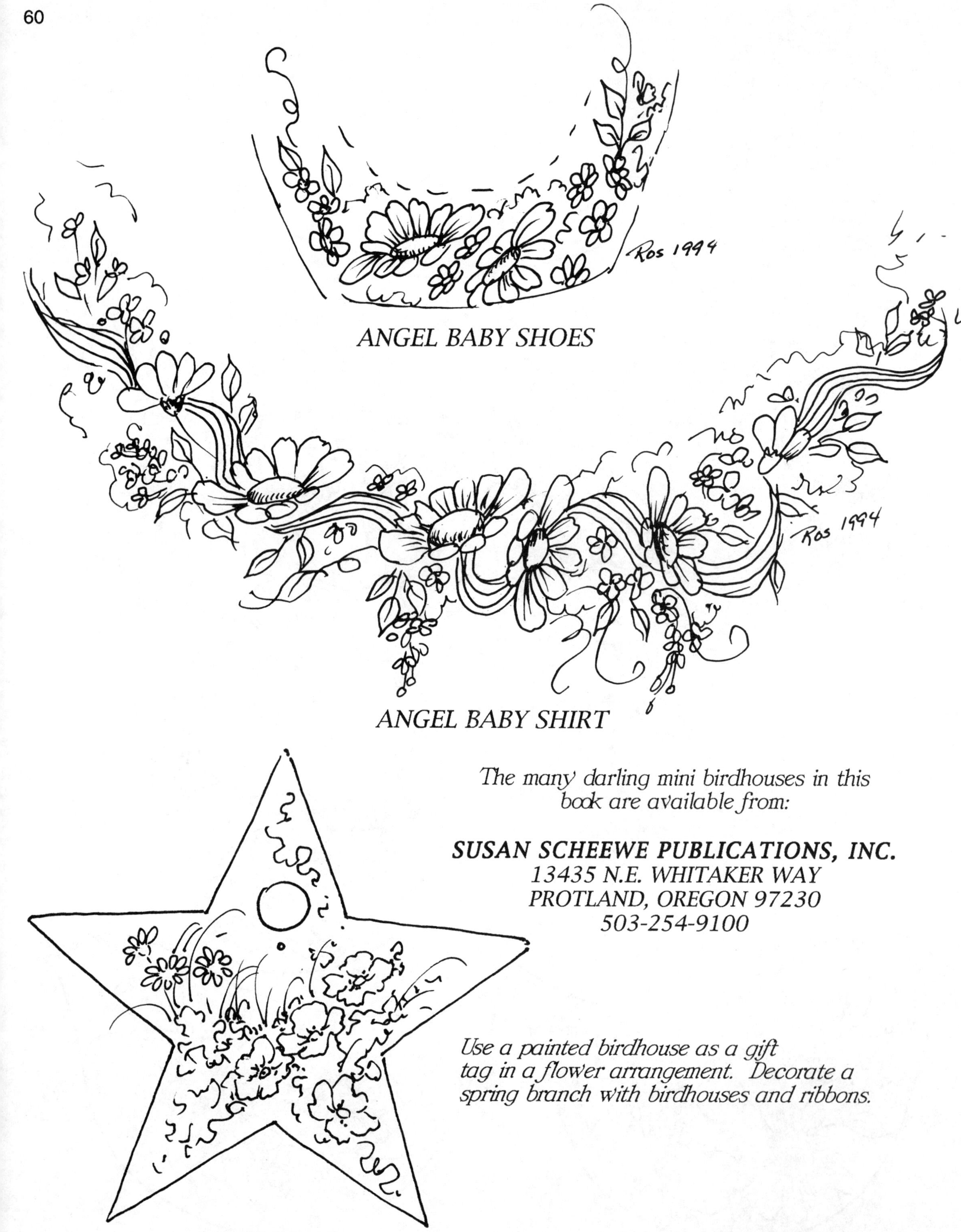

ANGEL BABY SHOES

ANGEL BABY SHIRT

The many darling mini birdhouses in this book are available from:

SUSAN SCHEEWE PUBLICATIONS, INC.
13435 N.E. WHITAKER WAY
PROTLAND, OREGON 97230
503-254-9100

Use a painted birdhouse as a gift tag in a flower arrangement. Decorate a spring branch with birdhouses and ribbons.

My husband Larry and I have had so much pleasure and love from our angel baby granddaughter. We hope you will want to paint designs for your special angel babies.
Ros 1994
ANGEL BABY OVERALLS

Baby Shirt

Surface:
White Sweatshirt.

Palette: (Grumbacher fabric dyes)
Marvelous
Violetta
Super Hide White
Comet Blue
Peacock Blue
Tulip Yellow
Dark Blue
India Green
Textile Medium
Lunar Lites
Textile Medium

Brushes:
#4 Filbert Brush
1/4 inch and 3/8 inch Angle Shader
.05 Pigma Pen

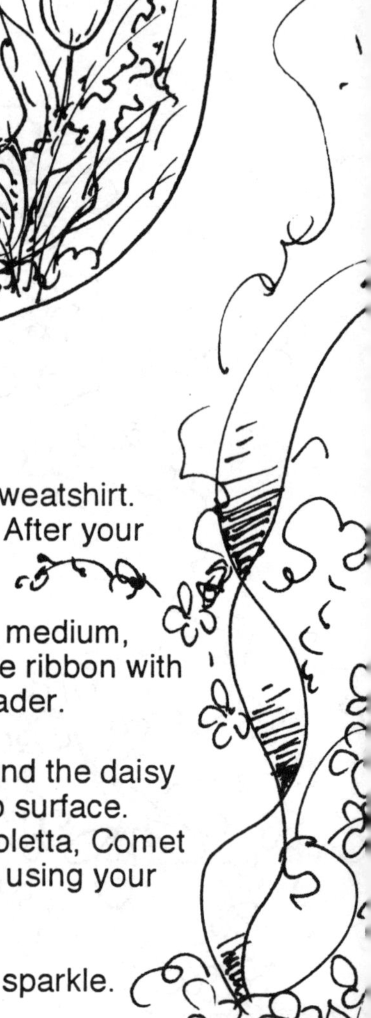

Pattern & Ink: Transfer pattern with tulle and charcoal pencil to sweatshirt. Ink design with Pigma Pen and add as many lines as pleases you. After your design is painted and dry draw more ink lines as desired.

Ribbon: Paint ribbon with Comet Blue and small amount of textile medium, using 3/8 inch angle shader. Leave the highlights white. Shade the ribbon with Peacock Blue and Dark Blue using just the corner of your angle shader.

Flowers & Foliage: Paint a small amount of textile medium around the daisy petals. Tap India Green foliage using your filbert brush on the damp surface. This will leave the daisy petals white. Tap lose filler flowers with Violetta, Comet Blue, and Super Hide White. Paint Daisy centers with Tulip Yellow using your filbert brush. Allow to dry.

Sparkle: Paint Lunar Lites on daisy petals and bow highlights for sparkle.

BABY SHIRT

Children are a special gift to the world to remind us of the essence of love. Show your love by painting a one of a kind garment for a young person in your family or for a friend.
Plus, what a delightful way to cover spots, spills or stains with a design.
To
From

My Garden

Surface:
Creations in Canvas Recipe File

Palette: (Deco Americana Acrylic)

Titanium White
Avocado
Olive Green
Evergreen
True Blue
Dioxazine Purple
Boysenberry Pink
Cad Yellow
Lavender
Burgundy Wine

Brushes:

Susie's Foliage Brush
#6 Round Brush
#1 Liner Brush

Boarders: Transfer pattern of boarders centered on recipe file with gray graphite. Mask boarders with masking tape. Paint Lavender outer boarder and allow to dry. Remove tape and re-tape for dark green background. Paint background with Evergreen and a little Dioxazine Purple. Line boarders with Burgundy Wine.

Background Foliage: Tap loose foliage with Avocado and Olive Green using Susie's Foliage Brush. Allow to dry.

Liriope: Pattern flowers and leaves as needed with white graphite. Paint Liriope with Avocado, Olive Green, and Titanium White, using your liner brush. Pick up some of all colors (do not mix) on your brush by pulling through the paint. Flick up wide blades of grass forming clumps (refer to worksheet).

Impatiens: Paint Impatiens with Boysenberry Pink and Titanium White using #6 round brush

Delphiniums & Daisies: Paint Delphiniums with pinks, blues and purples using the tip of your #6 round brush. Add little petal flowers on top with pink/purple and Super Hide White. Paint Daisy petals with Titanium White using your #2 round brush. Paint centers with Cad. Yellow.

Stems & Grasses: Paint little stems and grasses with Olive Green and a little water using your liner brush.

My Garden Watering Can

Surface:
Tin watering can same pattern as on recipe folder

Note: Refer to directions for *My Garden* recipe file for palette, brushes and directions.

Basecoat: Basecoat the watering can with two coats of Forest Green.

Flowers: Paint liriope, impatiens, and daises according to *My Garden.*

Crape Myrtle: Tap foliage for Crape Myrtle tree across the top of can with Evergreen, Avocado, and Olive Green using your foliage brush. Add branches with Dark Chocolate using your liner brush and a little water. Highlight branches with Dark Chocolate and Titanium White. Tap Crape Myrtle blossoms using Burgundy Wine, Boysenberry Pink and Titanium White using you foliage brush.

MY GARDEN (RECIPE FILE)

Be sure to use to use a permanent marker when pen and inking, if you don't the ink will run! oops.

BOUQUET VISOR

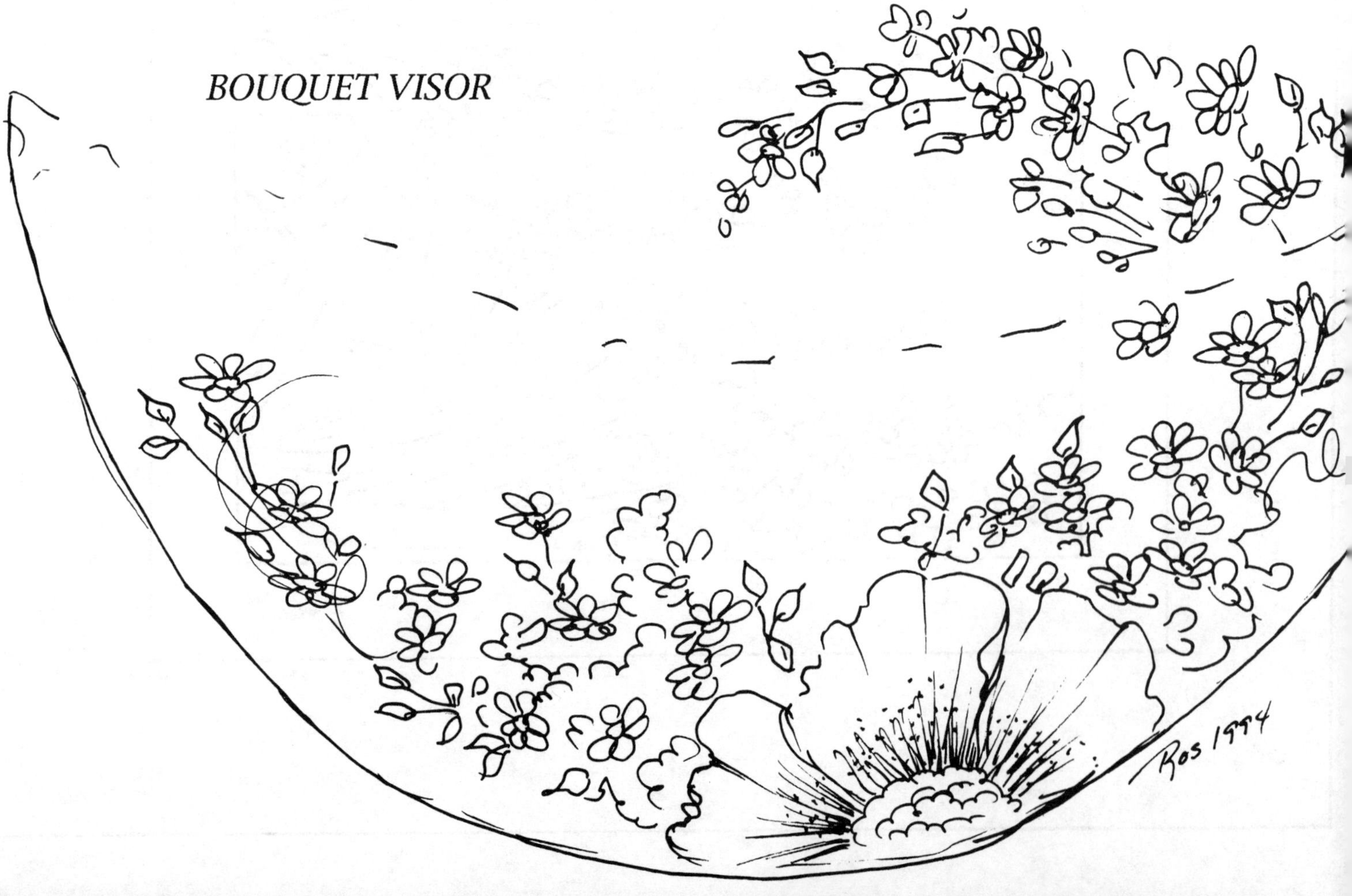

BOUQUET SUN HAT

This would work well on a summer T-shirt around the neck as well as a summer hat.

Bouquet

Surface:
White Knit Shirt, Shoes, Hat, Visor.

Palette: (Grumbacher fabric dyes)
Violetta
Comet Blue
Peacock Blue
Tulip Yellow
Magenta
India Green
Green Olive
Lunar Lites
Textile Medium

Brushes:
#4 Filbert Brush
1/2 inch Angle Shader
#1 Liner Brush
.05 Pigma Pen

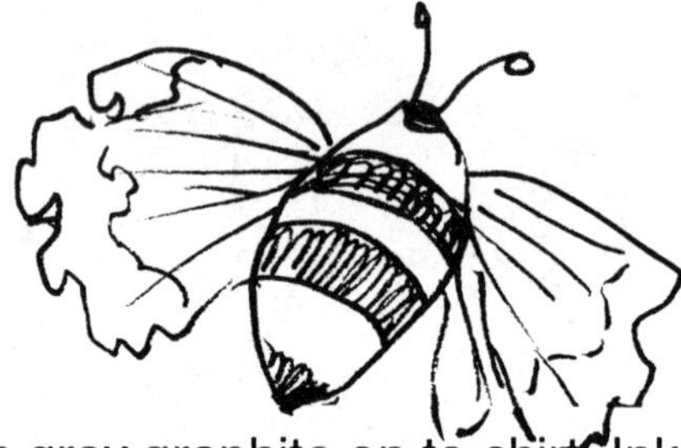

Patterning and Inking: Transfer pattern with gray graphite on to shirt. Ink design with Pigma Pen. Add as many detail lines as desired.

Blossoms: Paint large blossems with Magenta and angle shader. Paint each petal first with a little textile medium. While still wet pick up a small amount of Magenta on the point of the angle shader. Place color next to center of flower and pull streaks with the edge of the brush. Paint flower centers with Tulip Yellow and shade with a little Magenta.

Bell Flowers: Paint bell shaped flowers first with textile medium then with Violetta. Paint the darkest area at the stem end of each flower.

Leaves: Paint the large leaves with textile medium. Paint Green Olive along the vein of the leaf and down the opposite edge. Shade a few leaves with a touch of Violetta. Allow to dry.

Background Tint: Paint textile medium around large flowers and leaves. Using water in your paint tap filler flowers and background color with greens, blues, and violets. Leave daisy petals unpainted. Paint flower centers Tulip Yellow.

Bees: Paint bees with Tulip Yellow, and shade with Magenta and Tulip Yellow. Paint bee wings with Lunar Lites.

Grasses: Paint fine line grasses with India Green and water using your liner brush . Allow to dry. Add more ink lines if desired.

BOUQUET SHIRT

BOUQUET SHOES

RIGHT SHOE PATTERN SHOWN
REVERSE PATTERN FOR LEFT SHOE

BOUQUET SHIRT
Ros 1994

DAISY DOODLES & DABS

Ros
1994

Nothing is more inviting than a backyard blooming with summer flowers. Bring the pleasure of flowers indoors. This design could also be used around flowers pots or planters.

I love to wear hats and hope you will want to paint one for yourself. The same design would look great on a T-shirt or on a kitchen cabinet door.

DAISY HAT

DAISY GLOVES
FLOWER POT OR
BABY HAT
ROS 1994
ROS 1994

Daisy Garden Set

Surface:

Trowel, Gardening Gloves, Straw Hat, Lamp, and Flower Pot, Watering can

Palette: (Deco Americana Acrylic)

Titanium White
Avocado
Olive Green
Evergreen
Cad. Yellow
Burgundy Wine
Dioxazine Purple

Brushes:

#4 and 8 Filbert Brush
#20 Flat Shader
Susie's Foliage Brush
#1 Liner Brush

Basecoats and Patterns: Refer to general direction as to basecoatand patterning on various surfaces.

Foliage: Tap foliage on to surface with Evergreen, Avocado and Olive Green using Susie's' Foliage Brush. Allow to dry.

Daisies: Pattern Daisies and filler flowers as desired with white graphite. Paint Daisy petals with Titanium White using #8 filbert brush. Paint centers with Cad. Yellow and shade with Cad. Yellow mixed with a touch of Dioxazine Purple.

Filler Flowers: Tap filler flowers with Dioxazine Purple using your #4 filbert brush. Form little petals on these clusters with Dioxazine Purple and Titanium White.

Blossoms: Paint blossoms with Burgundy Wine using #8 filbert brush. Highlight petals by flicking from the edge of the petal toward the center of the flower with Titanium White.

Stems & Squiggles: Paint stems and squiggles with Avocado using you Liner Brush and a little water.

Susan Scheewe Publications, Inc.

ACRYLIC BOOKS

	Vol.	Title	No.	Price
	Vol. 19	"Gift of Painting" by Susan Scheewe	230	$9.50____
	Vol. 1	"Painting It's Our Bag" by Bev Hink/Susan Scheewe	193	$9.50____
	Vol. 4	"Keepsake Sampler" by Susan & Camille Scheewe	200	$9.50____
	Vol. 1	"Loving You" by Susan & Camille Scheewe	244	$9.50____
	Vol. 1	"Keepsakes For The Holidays" by Charleen Stempel & Susan Scheewe	286	$9.50____
	Vol. 1	"Mrs. MacGregor's Garden" by Charleen Stempel & Susan Scheewe	316	$9.50____
*NEW	Vol. 1	"Country Heartworks" by Reed Baxter	352	$9.50____
	Vol. 1	"Kids And Water" by Joyce Benner	234	$9.50____
	Vol. 2	"The Flower Market" by Joyce Benner	319	$9.50____
	Vol. 1	"Country Fixin's" by Rhonda Caldwell	307	$9.50____
	Vol. 2	"Country Fixin's - Sunflower Friends" by Rhonda Caldwell	321	$9.50____
	Vol. 3	"Country Fixin's - For All Seasons" by Rhonda Caldwell	332	$9.50____
*NEW	Vol. 1	"A Painters Garden" by Jane Dillon	354	$9.50____
	Vol. 1	"Santas and Sams" by Bobi Dolara	258	$9.50____
	Vol. 2	"Vintage Peace" by Bobi Dolara	270	$9.50____
	Vol. 1	"Floral Designs" by Carol Empet	312	$9.50____
	Vol. 2	"Floral Designs 2" by Carol Empet	338	$9.50____
	Vol. 1	"Romantically Tole Bauernmalerei" by Sherry Gall	311	$9.50____
	Vol. 1	"Holiday Gathering" by Angie Hupp	267	$9.50____
	Vol. 3	"Heavenly Gathering" by Angie Hupp	320	$9.50____
	Vol. 1	"Happy Heart, Happy Home" by Cathy Jones	241	$9.50____
	Vol. 1	"Pickets & Pastimes" by Marie & Jim King	329	$9.50____
*NEW	Vol. 2	"Pickets & Pastimes 2, Heart of The Seasons" by Marie & Jim King	348	$9.50____
	Vol. 1	"Huckleberry Horse" by Hanna Long	269	$9.50____
	Vol. 2	"Love Lives Here" by Mary Lynn Lewis	185	$6.50____
	Vol. 3	"Love Lives Here" by Mary Lynn Lewis	195	$6.50____
	Vol. 1	"Special Welcomes" by Corinne Miller	287	$9.50____
	Vol. 2	"Special Welcomes" by Corinne Miller	298	$9.50____
	Vol. 3	"Special Welcomes #3, Crazy About Crafting" by Corinne Miller	309	$9.50____
	Vol. 4	"Special Welcomes #4 Farm-N-Friends" by Corinne Miller	324	$9.50____
	Vol. 5	"Special Welcomes #5 All Wrapped Up" by Corinne Miller	333	$9.50____
*NEW	Vol. 6	"Special Welcomes #6 Crop Keepers" by Corinne Miller	347	$9.50____
	Vol. 1	"Change With The Seasons, Wire Loops" by Joanna Miller	331	$9.50____
	Vol. 1	"Fruit & Flower Fantasies" by Joyce Morrison	277	$9.50____
	Vol. 1	"Wildflower Sampler" by Bev Norman	191	$9.50____
	Vol. 1	"Whimsical Critters" by Lori Ohlson	228	$7.50____
	Vol. 2	"Sunflower Farm" by Lori Ohlson	326	$9.50____
	Vol. 1	"Holiday Medley" by Nina Owens	265	$9.50____
	Vol. 2	"Another Holiday Medley" by Nina Owens	296	$9.50____
	Vol. 1	"Oh Those Little Rascals" by Diane Permenter	247	$9.50____
	Vol. 6	"Acrylic Charms" by Sharon Rachal	305	$9.50____
	Vol. 1	"Forever In My Heart" by Diane Richards.....AC/Fabric	188	$6.50____
	Vol. 2	"Memories In My Heart" by Diane Richards.....AC/Fabric	189	$6.50____
	Vol. 3	"Forever In My Heart II" by Diane Richards.....AC/Fabric	205	$9.50____
	Vol. 6	"Angels In My Stocking" by Diane Richards	254	$9.50____
	Vol. 7	"Nostalgic Dreams" by Diane Richards	273	$9.50____
*NEW	Vol. 8	"Angel Kisses" by Diane Richards	346	$9.50____
	Vol. 1	"Holiday Hangarounds" by Marsha Sellers	327	$9.50____
	Vol. 1	"Creations In Canvas...and More" by Carol Spooner	256	$9.50____
	Vol. 1	"Gran's Garden" by Ros Stallcup	295	$9.50____
	Vol. 2	"Another Gran's Garden" by Ros Stallcup	315	$9.50____
	Vol. 3	"Gran's Garden & House" by Ros Stallcup	334	$9.50____
*NEW	Vol. 4	"Gran's Garden Party" by Ros Stallcup	345	$9.50____
	Vol. 1	"Christmas Greetings from the Cottage" by Chris Stokes	336	$9.50____
	Vol. 1	"Christmas Visions" by Max Terry	285	$9.50____
	Vol. 3	"Painting Clay Pot-pourri" by Max Terry	310	$9.50____
	Vol. 1	"Country Primitives" by Maxine Thomas	274	$9.50____
	Vol. 2	"Country Primitives 2" by Maxine Thomas	300	$9.50____
	Vol. 3	"Country Primitives 3" by Maxine Thomas	322	$9.50____
*NEW	Vol. 4	"Country Primitives 4" by Maxine Thomas	350	$9.50____
	Vol. 1	"Rise & Shine" by Jolene Thompson	214	$6.50____
	Vol. 2	"Garden Gate" by Jolene Thompson	250	$9.50____
	Vol. 5	"Count Your Blessings" by Chris Thornton	213	$9.50____
	Vol. 6	"Share Your Blessings" by Chris Thornton	226	$9.50____
	Vol. 7	"Blessings" by Chris Thornton	255	$9.50____
	Vol. 8	"Christmas Blessings" by Chris Thornton	266	$9.50____
	Vol. 9	"Blessings For The Home" by Chris Thornton	275	$9.50____
	Vol. 10	"Bazaar Blessings" by Chris Thornton	299	$9.50____
	Vol. 11	"Painted Blessings" by Chris Thornton	323	$9.50____
*NEW	Vol. 12	"Family Blessings" by Chris Thornton	349	$9.50____
*NEW	Vol. 13	"Summer Blessings" by Chris Thornton	356	$9.50____
	Vol. 1	"Watermelon Wedges and Rustic Edges" by Lorinne Thurlow	342	$9.50____
*NEW	Vol. 2	"Watermelon Wedges and Rustic Edges 2" by Lorinne Thurlow	353	$9.50____
	Vol. 1	"Barnyard Friends" by Lou Ann Trice	306	$9.50____
	Vol. 5	"Daydreams & Sweet Shirts II" by Don & Lynn Weed	208	$9.50____
	Vol. 1	"Connie's Favorite Old-Time Labels" by Connie Williams	335	$9.50____
*NEW	Vol. 2	"Connie's Garden Seed Packets" by Connie Williams	351	$9.50____
	Vol. 1	"Floral Fabrics and Watercolor" by Sally Williams	262	$9.50____
	Vol. 1	"A Time For Giving" by Evelyn Wright	308	$9.50____

****

SHIPPING & HANDLING CHARGES

Add $2.50 for the First Book for shipping and handling.

Add $1.50 per each additional book.

Please Add $3.00 for handling & postage. PER TAPES. Sorry we must have a "NO RE-FUND - NO RETURN" policy.

U.S CURRENCY

PRICES SUBJECT TO CHANGE WITHOUT NOTICE

FOR MORE INFORMATION ON BOOKS OR SUPPLIES CALL OR WRITE US

WE ARE ALWAYS GLAD TO HEAR FROM YOU!

5-14-96

13435 N.E. Whitaker Way Portland, Or. 97230 PH (503) 254-9100 FAX (503) 252-9508

WATERCOLOR BOOKS

	Vol.	Title	No.	Price	
	Vol. 20	"Simply Country Watercolors" by Susan Scheewe Brown	257	$9.50	___
	Vol. 21	"Simply Watercolor" by Susan Scheewe Brown.....T.V. Book	260	$11.95	___
	Vol. 22	"Watercolor For Everyone" by Susan Scheewe Brown.....T.V. Book	276	$11.95	___
	Vol. 23	"Watercolor Step by Step" by Susan Scheewe Brown.....T.V. Book	294	$11.95	___
	Vol. 24	"Introduction to Watercolor" by Susan Scheewe Brown.....T.V. Book	314	$11.95	___
	Vol. 25	"Watercolors Anyone Can Paint" by Susan Scheewe Brown...T.V. Book	325	$11.95	___
*NEW	Vol. 26	"Watercolor - The Garden Scene" by Susan Scheewe Brown... T.V. Book	339	$11.95	___
	Vol. 4	"Enjoy Watercolor" by Ellie Cook	210	$7.50	___
	Vol. 6	"Watercolor Memories" by Ellie Cook	246	$9.50	___
	Vol. 3	"Watercolor Made Easy 3" by Kathy George	301	$9.50	___
	Vol. 1	"The Way I Started" by Gary Hawk	120	$6.00	___
	Vol. 2	"Anyone Can Watercolor" by Ken Johnson	118	$6.50	___
	Vol. 1	"Watercolor Fun & Easy" by Beverly Kaiser	243	$7.50	___
	Vol. 1	"Flowers, Ribbon and Lace in Watercolor" by Linda McCulloch	280	$9.50	___

PEN & INK BOOKS / COLORED PENCIL BOOKS

Vol.	Title	No.	Price	
Vol. 6	"Journey of Memories" by Claudia Nice	166	$6.50	___
Vol. 7	"Scenes from Seasons Past" by Claudia Nice	183	$9.50	___
Vol. 8	"Taste of Summer" by Claudia Nice	223	$9.50	___
Vol. 9	"Familiar Faces" by Claudia Nice	284	$9.50	___
Vol. 2	"Colored Pencil Made Easy" by Jane Wunder	242	$7.50	___
Vol. 3	"The Beauty of Colored Pencil and Ink Drawing" by Jane Wunder	259	$7.50	___

VIDEOS BY SUSAN SCHEEWE BROWN

"The Gift Of Painting Simply Watercolor" 60 Minutes	$24.95	___
"The Gift Of Painting" 90 Minutes	$24.95	___
"Paintings For The Holidays" 60 Minutes	$24.95	___
"Watercolor & Oil Do Mix" 60 Minutes	$24.95	___
"Watercolor Special Effects" 60 Minutes	$24.95	___
"Fabric Painting Fun" 60 Minutes	$24.95	___

NAME ___

ADDRESS ___

CITY/STATE/ZIP ___

PH( ) ___

VISA ___

M/C ___

EXP. DATE ___

SHIPPING $ ___

SHIP TO ___

OILS BOOKS

Vol.	Title	No.	Price	
Vol. 1	"His and Hers" by Susan Scheewe	101	$6.50	___
Vol. 7	"Paint 'n Patch" by Susan Scheewe	107	$5.50	___
Vol. 11	"I Love To Paint" by Susan Scheewe	111	$6.50	___
Vol. 14	"Enjoy Painting Animals" by Susan Scheewe	114	$6.50	___
Vol. 19	"Gift Of Painting" by Susan Scheewe O/AC/WC	230	$9.50	___
Vol. 1	"Western Images" by Becky Anthony	186	$6.50	___
Vol. 3	"Fantasy Flowers II" by Georgia Bartlett	129	$6.50	___
Vol. 5	"Soft Petals" by Georgia Bartlett	171	$6.50	___
Vol. 6	"Painting Fantasy Flowers" by Georgia Bartlett	215	$7.50	___
Vol. 7	"Flowers" by Georgia Bartlett	290	$9.50	___
Vol. 8	"Petals" by Georgia Bartlett	317	$9.50	___
Vol. 9	"Floral Medley" by Georgia Bartlett *NEW	344	$9.50	___
Vol. 3	"Barnscapes & More" by Donna Bell	218	$9.50	___
Vol. 4	"Countryscapes" by Donna Bell	249	$9.50	___
Vol. 5	"Painter to Painter" by Donna Bell	263	$9.50	___
Vol. 6	"Landscapes With Acrylics & Oil" by Donna Bell	282	$9.50	___
Vol. 1	"Natures Palette" by Carol Binford.....O/AC	248	$9.50	___
Vol. 2	"Oil Painting The Easy Way" by Bill Blackman	337	$9.50	___
Vol. 3	"Lighted Windows & Gardens" by Bill Blackman *NEW	355	$9.50	___
Vol. 1	"Mini Mini More" by Terri and Nancy Brown	150	$9.50	___
Vol. 2	"Mini Mini More" by Terri and Nancy Brown	151	$9.50	___
Vol. 4	"Heritage Trails" by Terri and Nancy Brown	169	$6.50	___
Vol. 6	"Garden Trails" by Terri and Nancy Brown	283	$9.50	___
Vol. 2	"Windows of My World" by Jackie Claflin	181	$9.50	___
Vol. 3	"Windows of My World 3" by Jackie Claflin	303	$9.50	___
Vol. 4	"Expressions In Oil" by Delores Egger	239	$7.50	___
Vol. 1	"Victorian Days" by Gloria Gaffney	240	$9.50	___
Vol. 2	"Days of Heaven" by Gloria Gaffney	252	$9.50	___
Vol. 3	"Winter Song" by Gloria Gaffney	271	$9.50	___
Vol. 1	"Roses Are For Everyone" by Bill Huffaker	145	$7.50	___
Vol. 3	"Nature's Beauty" by Bill Huffaker	177	$6.50	___
Vol. 1	"Copper, Silver, Brass & Glass" by Susan Jenkins	211	$6.50	___
Vol. 1	"In Full Bloom" by Susan Jenkins	313	$9.50	___
Vol. 1	"Backroads of My Memory" by Geri Kisner	225	$9.50	___
Vol. 2	"Backroads of My Memory" by Geri Kisner	245	$9.50	___
Vol. 1	"Ducks and Geese" by Jean Lyles	172	$6.50	___
Vol. 1	"Raining Cats & Dogs" by Todd Mallett	304	$9.50	___
Vol. 1	"Pathway To Painting" by Lee McGowan	281	$9.50	___
Vol. 2	"Another Path To Follow" by Lee McGowen	328	$9.50	___
Vol. 1	"Bitterroot Backroads" by Glenice Moore	330	$9.50	___
Vol. 2	"Bitteroot Backroads 2" by Glenice Moore	340	$9.50	___
Vol. 1	"Stepping Stones" by Judy Nutter *NEW	121	$6.50	___
Vol. 1	"Painting with Paulson" by Buck Paulson	343	$11.95	___
Vol. 1	"Rustic Charms" by Sharon Rachal *NEW	175	$6.50	___
Vol. 2	"Rustic Charms II" by Sharon Rachal	199	$9.50	___
Vol. 3	"Rustic Charms III" by Sharon Rachal	217	$6.50	___
Vol. 4	"Rustic Charms IV" by Sharon Rachal	238	$7.50	___
Vol. 5	"Rustic Charms V, Florals" by Sharon Rachal	261	$9.50	___
Vol. 1	"Painting Flowers With Augie" by Augie Reis	152	$6.50	___
Vol. 3	"Realistic Technique" by Judy Sleight	341	$9.50	___
Vol. 1	"Soft & Misty Paintings" by Kathy Snider *NEW	204	$9.50	___
Vol. 2	"Soft & Misty Paintings"by Kathy Snider	229	$9.50	___
Vol. 4	"Friends We've Known" by Gene Waggoner	187	$7.50	___
Vol. 5	"Friends Are Forever" by Gene Waggoner	231	$7.50	___
Vol. 1	"Fantasy Folk" by Don Weed	123	$6.50	___
Vol. 2	"Painting The Clowns" by Don Weed	124	$6.50	___
Vol. 1	"Something Special For Everyone" by Mildred Yeiser	158	$6.50	___
Vol. 2	"Something Special For Everyone" by Mildred Yeiser	178	$6.50	___
Vol. 5	"Soft & Gentle Paintings" by Mildred Yeiser	268	$9.50	___

Susan Scheewe Publications Inc.

13435 N.E. Whitaker Way Portland, Or. 97230 PH (503) 254-9100 FAX (503) 252-9508

GRAPE BASKET &
GRAPE TOTE BOX
Pages 23, 24, 25, 26, 27

DELPHINUIM RECIPE BOX
Pages 34, 35

DELPHINIUM CROCK LID
Page 35

WELCOME TO MY GARDEN
Pages 52, 53, 54, 55

SPRING TIME HOME
Pages 14, 15, 16